Lucy Fait

Mother to Hundreds

Lucy Faithfull

Mother to Hundreds

Judith Niechcial

CONTENTS

ILLUSTRATIONS

FOREWORD

I am pleased to write this foreword for two reasons. First, because it is a compelling account of a remarkable woman in the context of her family, her class, her social milieu and very troubled times, spanning nearly a century and two world wars. Secondly, it sheds more light, through careful inquiry, on the development of social work, especially child welfare over a substantial period. Putting this story into a historical context is very important. I am very grateful to Judith Niechcial for bringing this material together in such an accessible form.

As I read these pages, I recognise the woman I knew as Children's Officer for Oxford City whom I liked and respected and whose warm and engaging personality made it so easy for me to work with her. But I also learnt in much more detail the extent of her contribution to social welfare over the years. In particular, there are three aspects of her work, in addition to the better known, excellent Children's Department in the 1960s, her main achievement, which make for fascinating reading. One is her significant involvement in the mass evacuation of children during the Second World War. Only recently have we begun to see more comment in the press and media on this important and traumatic aspect of the War. Lucy's views, as well as her work on this, were significant. She never fell victim to the temptations of a sentimental 'rescue motive'. Fast forward to the later days of her life as a Tory peer, and we see an unfaltering determination to secure a better deal for deprived children – often in a hostile climate and even when it meant opposing party policy. Food for thought as we move to abolish the House of Lords in its present form! Lastly, and even more remarkable, was her work towards provision of treatment for sex offenders against children (Her 'Lucy Faithfull Foundation' is a legacy of this). Given her age and background and the unpopularity of that cause, this tells one something very important about her courage and values.

I have recently reread a biography by the late Kay Jones on Dame Eileen Younghusband, whose career spanned much the same period. Lucy's story reminds us again of the extraordinary journeys these women took, in the steps of their famous Victorian sisters, from privilege, (though not in Lucy's case affluence), and the security of upper middle class assumptions to profound involvement in the alleviation of poverty and its associated ills. This was often at great personal cost, but undertaken with enormous energy and commitment. Lucy's childhood was full of uncertainty and pain, though there was also much love. Her father was killed in the First World War, before she was of school age; she went to boarding school at seven, a separation from her mother and brother which deeply affected her – "I couldn't eat, I couldn't talk, I couldn't move". These experiences were taken in and used throughout her life, successfully sublimated in her work for children and their parents. She was also the ultimate 'networker', unashamedly using any contacts, from the socially elite and professionally distinguished to important people in children's lives, to achieve her (wholly admirable) ends.

In short, this book helps those who did not know her to understand why those of us who did have such warm and lively memories, not of a saint, but of a real and good person in and of her time. Our society is the better for her life.

As we struggle through the present difficulties in caring for disadvantaged children, this reminder of earlier times is welcome. We need to find a way of recapturing some of the energy and optimism so characteristic of the early post war years, despite its hardships. I think that Lucy would have agreed with the title of an article of mine written in 1998 - two years after her death – 'It was more difficult than we thought'. But she would never have been defeated.

Olive Stevenson. Professor Emeritus,
University of Nottingham

References:

Jones, Kay, "Eileen Younghusband. A biography", in *Occasional Papers in Social Administration*, No. 76, (London: Bedford Square Press, 1984).

Stevenson, Olive, "It was more difficult than we thought; a reflection on 30 years of child welfare practice", in *Child and Family Social Work*, Vol. 3, Issue 3, 1998.

Lucy Faithfull: mother to hundreds

INTRODUCTION

Lucy Faithfull, later Baroness Faithfull of Wolvercote, OBE, (1910–1996) was a committed social worker, a life-long and passionate campaigner for children, and a vociferous member of the House of Lords. An account of her life is a history of child care in the twentieth century. She was a Tory life peeress, but she opposed, and persuaded others to oppose, so many of the measures that the party supported in relation to the welfare of children, that the Tory whips gave her the nickname of 'Lady Faithless'.[1]

She never married or had children of her own, but she made a difference, directly or indirectly, to the lives of very many children and families. She also realized very early on that, in order to reunite families where sexual abuse had taken place, and to protect children from further abuse, effective treatment of the abusers was necessary, and gave her name to the Faithfull Foundation, which must have been the least 'cuddly' charity of the 1990s.

I chose her as the subject for two reasons: first, because of my admiration for her as a woman and for her work, and, second, because there are so few biographical studies of social workers. Writing about literary figures, actors and film stars, soldiers and heroic adventurers seems to command the biography market and hold public attention. Public servants of whatever type are seen perhaps as mere plodders, working away at the margins of society with unglamorous people as their clients, without brilliant friends, maybe even as not particularly intelligent. In fact social work is one of the most fascinating, involving and contentious occupations, and Lucy Faithfull one of its most admired and respected practitioners among those working in the twentieth century.

There are several reasons why social work is an ignored and devalued profession. It does not command an exclusive body of knowledge in the same way as the medical or legal professions do.

> Because social work arises in response to problems of everyday living, its expertise rests in gaining a thorough and sensitive understanding of ordinary matters. Its language sounds familiar to everyone (so) […] it has difficulty in claiming a monopoly of skill or even roughly exclusive jurisdiction of its working environment. To the onlooker, the practices of social workers do not appear markedly different from those of ordinary social intercourse.[2]

It also is seen as a largely female area of work.

> The overwhelming majority of British social workers were women, direct descendents of the middle-class 'do-gooding' lady almoners of the hospitals and voluntary 'Care Committees' workers of the 1930s–1950s. In its preoccupation with child development and concentration on the emotional and practical needs of those in distress, social work appeared to reinforce at a social level the stereotype of domestic 'women's work', vacating the higher ground of academia, and medical prestige to men.[3]

Lucy Faithfull never described herself as a feminist. She was born too late to be a suffragette and too early to be involved in the women's movement of the late 1960s. She flourished in the female environments in which she grew up and worked for much of her life, but emerged into the male-dominated worlds of Social Services Departments and was the first social worker of either gender to sit in the House of Lords. She was, in many ways, a woman of her time, her life being influenced and shaped by a succession of wars, from the Boer War to the Second World War.

Lucy worked both in the civil service and a local authority. She commanded the affection of people she worked with, from the most neglected or lonely child to the Archbishops and millionaires she was involved with in later years. She was equally warm and valuing of everyone she came into contact with, be they small children, young offenders, waitresses, or eminent politicians.

She was not a well-organised person. I was privileged to be given access to her archive at St Hilda's College, Oxford, which had not yet been catalogued; in fact, it was "untouched", in the words of the archivist. It was chaotic, the labels on files often bearing little relation to their contents, with much duplication of material, and containing sheaves of documents in Lucy's almost illegible hand-writing. For a brief period she employed a secretary to work for her in Oxford, but even this person's filing system followed no logic that I could discern. This all made for a labour-intensive period of research for me.

Although both Rebecca Abrams and Bob Holman have made tape recordings of conversations with Lucy, and used these in their respective books (see bibliography), there is, as yet, no full biography of Baroness Faithfull. Four aspects of her life are particularly significant, and form the framework of four chapters: first, her early work with evacuees during the Second World War, which formed the basis of her thinking about the needs of children and her motivation for pursuing a career in social work; second, her time as Children's Officer for the City of Oxford, a department that had a reputation as a centre of child care excellence; third, her pioneering work in the field of residential treatment and rehabilitation of sex offenders, a controversial area of work; and, fourth, her energetic post-retirement career as a life peer in the House of Lords where she carried forward her mission to be champion for social work in general, and children in particular. Other chapters highlight her formative years as an almost parentless child, her work as a Home Office inspector, her time as a Director of Social Services, her devout but quiet Anglicanism, and the many campaigns and aspects of social policy in which she was passionately involved, for example therapeutic residential care for children, inter-country adoption, early years provision, and the treatment of young offenders in the criminal justice system.

For the sake of brevity, and also because, as biographers do, I have come to feel I know her intimately, I shall refer to her as 'Lucy'. Even though this might seem over-familiar, I think it is preferable to the pompous term, 'Baroness Faithfull' or worse, the masculine 'Faithfull'.

Notes:

[1] John Rea Price, (2004), 'Faithfull, Lucy, Baroness Faithfull (1910–1996)', *Oxford Dictionary of National Biography*, (Oxford: OUP).

[2] David Howe in Joel Kanter (ed.) *Face to Face with Children – The Life and Work of Clare Winnicott.* (London: Karnac, 2004) p. 117.

[3] Holmes, Jeremy, in Joel Kanter, *Face to Face with Children.*

ACKNOWLEDGMENTS

My especial thanks are due to Elizabeth Boardman and Maria Croghan of the Archive and Library of St. Hilda's College, Oxford for allowing me to spend long hours and days in their offices going through the many boxes of Lucy Faithfull's papers. It was Dr. Ann Buchanan, Fellow of St. Hilda's, who went to Lucy's house after her death at the request of her executors, cleared her possessions and physically rescued her extremely disorganised papers, and persuaded St. Hilda's to house them.[1]

Rebecca Abrams made recordings, and transcriptions of her tapes, of two interviews with Lucy Faithfull in 1989 and 1990, which she used in her book, *Woman in a Man's World*.[2] She has deposited them in the National Sound Archive at the British Library, where I went to hear Lucy's beautifully modulated, upper class voice. As Lucy herself said, "You are a very good interviewer". Rebecca, thank you.

Antoine Rogers of Birmingham Settlement lent me minutes and records of the Settlement in the 1930s.

I never knew Lucy Faithfull, but so many people who had known her both personally and professionally generously allowed me to interview them. She had touched many lives, and more than a decade after her death, memories were vivid.

Bob Holman spoke with her about her work with evacuees and as Children's Officer in Oxford. Dr. Ron Davie and Peter Smith both worked with her as chair of the All-Party Parliamentary Group for Children. Keith Bilton of the Social Work History

Network also knew her in that context, and also gave me the source of the ballad, 'Other People's Babies'.

The Civil Servant Rupert Hughes recalled her work on the passage of the Children Act 1989 through the House of Lords. Professor Jane Tunstill of Royal Holloway, London University was with Lucy when she collapsed at the House of Lords, and she and Professor Jane Aldgate of the Open University shared their memories of travelling with her by train from Totnes. Simon Rodway and James King told me about her involvement with the Caldecott Community, and Ray Wyre, Hilary Eldridge and Adrianne Jones remembered her as Trustee of the Gracewell Institute and the Faithfull Foundation.

Several people who worked with Lucy at Oxford Children's Department, notably Jenny Fells, her one-time Deputy, and Don Brand, shared their memories of that time. Don convened a meeting with other Oxford staff, Joan Warren, Joan Glyn-Jones and Ann Thompson, and taped their conversation for me. Fiona Mackey sent me two letters from Lucy.

Lucy's close friends, Malcolm and Sheila Gough, were an invaluable source of information about Lucy's private life, and Malcolm, whom Lucy had wanted to be executor of her estate, generously shared with me a number of documents and photographs in his possession.

Drew Clode, who interviewed Lucy for the ADSS journal, 'Inform' kindly sent me his tape recording.

I am particularly grateful to the following peers who have invited me with courtesy to the House of Lords; Lord Mackay of Clashfern, Lady Nora David, and Lady Daphne Park. Lady Virginia Bottomley and Lady Valerie Howarth have answered correspondence.

Carl Boardman of Oxfordshire County Archive has tirelessly sifted through confidential Children's Department and Social Services Department records and allowed me to read minutes. The staff of the archives of the House of Lords, the London Metropolitan Archive, the National Archives at Kew, the Modern

Records Centre at the University of Warwick, the British Film Institute, the Imperial War Museum and the library of the National Children's Bureau have also been most helpful.

Ann Hart kindly showed me around what had been Lucy's house in North Oxford, and Clive Tilbrook explained the changes that Leigh Faithfull had made to his country cottage in East Meon, Hampshire.

I have also spoken or corresponded with Nanette Borrie, Judge Quentin Campbell, Dick Clough, Hugh Faithfull, Rachel Hodgkin, Jilly and Stuart Holden, Pat Laurie, Anna Martin, Canon Brian Mountford, Terry Philpot, John Rea Price, Daphne Statham, Professor Olive Stevenson, Professor June Thoburn, Sir William Utting, and Tom White.

Karen Thomas and Trish Carn worked tirelessly to turn my untidy manuscript into a publishable book.

To all these people I owe grateful thanks, and any errors or misrepresentations in this account of Lucy's life are mine alone.

1 They have now been professionally catalogued by Penelope Baker, with funds donated for the purpose by many donors who knew Lucy, notably Sir Evelyn Rothschild.
2 Rebecca Abrams, *Woman in a Man's World: Pioneering career women of the twentieth century* (London: Methuen, 1993).

CHAPTER ONE

SEPARATION AND SETTLEMENT

The photograph shows him as an exceptionally handsome man, with straight eyebrows and a firm chin. He is wearing the smart army uniform in which so many young men were proudly photographed before setting off into the mud and chaos of the First World War. His name is Sidney Leigh Faithfull, 2nd Lieutenant Royal Engineers, and he is Lucy Faithfull's father. His commission, an impressive scroll,[1] is dated 25 June 1916. As he was a mining engineer he was allocated to the 256th Tunnelling

Sidney Leigh Faithfull, Lucy's father

Company. It was to be a painfully short commission. Less than two months later, he was dead, "of the effects of gas at Arras", says a pencilled note on the back of his photo. I doubt if the even more impressive bronze medal, inscribed "He died for freedom and honour", and a note from King George was of any consolation to Bessie, his widow, left with two small children and homeless.

Sidney and Bessie were both English, but had met in South

Africa where Sidney had gone to work as a mining engineer and Bessie to join a brother who had TB and had been advised to move to a warm climate. Bessie trained as a nurse in Cape Town, and she and Sidney married in 1910 at Mafeking. Little Lucy was born just over eight months later at Wes Deep Mine, Boksburg, just east of Johannesburg. She was born a month prematurely, a fact that Bessie later said must explain Lucy's tendency to push herself forward. Sidney's income as a mines inspector was not great and there was no family money so, although comfortable, the family were not wealthy in the context of the times. This is how Lucy describes her early childhood:[2]

> We lived in a long, low bungalow looking onto a lake. One of the things that I remember was playing on the balcony and looking across and seeing a lot of men practising at a shooting range, and saying to my mother, 'Why are those men shooting?' And she said, 'Oh, they have to practise, because you know there are wars.' That always lived in my memory. My life seems to have been dominated first by the Boer War, then by the Great War, and then by the Second World War.
>
> My father was the chief inspector of mines and had a wide circle of friends, and my uncle had been town clerk of Mafeking and he used to come with his friends, and I remember the house with an enormous number of people coming and going. Of course, entertaining was easy because you had the staff, as everybody did in those days out in South Africa. We had two or three staff and we had the most marvellous 'boy', as they were called, Twopence, and he was the gardener and general handyman and lived in a hut in the garden. I absolutely loved Twopence, I used to follow him around.

However, this colonial childhood idyll was not to last. When War broke out, Sidney initially fought in the South African campaign before deciding, when it became clear that the situation was so dire in France, to travel to Europe to join the Western Front. Lucy remembers being aged six and standing on the quay waving him off on the troop ship, her last sight of him. Bessie, by this time, had a second child, Lucy's younger brother John Leigh, born in 1913. Left alone with two small children, Bessie decided to sell the bungalow and to take Lucy and Leigh, as he was always called, to England, with the idea of being able to see Sidney whenever he came home on leave. The little family lodged with an uncle and aunt in Newport, Monmouth, but Sidney never did have time to take any leave. Indecently soon, the telegram dreaded by so many thousands of families arrived on the doorstep announcing his death at the Battle of Arras.

Lucy describes her mother, and her bereavement:

> She was a most outstanding person. I mean, you're a widow, you've only been married five years, you're left with a pension of 207 pounds[3] a year and you bring up two children and send them to good schools, and me to university and my brother to be a solicitor [...] she was small and very delicate and very attractive. She was always enchanting, and she was always deeply loving and considerate, but she had that incredibly sad look. I used to look at her, and wish that she wasn't quite so sad. She never let it impinge on us if she could help it but it was inevitable.[4]

Lucy paints a desolate picture of life in Newport:

> The men that [mother] had known in Africa, and the husbands and brothers of her friends in Africa, used to come and spend their leaves with us. And then I remember as a small child, one by one they didn't return. And I said to her 'Why doesn't Uncle Jim [...] why doesn't this [...] come back?' And of course one by one they were killed. So that, in those early years one was really dominated by this war, when people just didn't return.[5]

Bessie prided herself on managing on a tight budget, and refused to apply to any organisation that might have helped out,[6] an attitude that Lucy admired and which I am sure influenced her belief that the aim of social policy should be to help the needy to help themselves. A condolence letter that Lucy received after her mother's death from someone signing herself "A" also remembers Bessie in 1915:

> She really was amazing the way she stood up to life then and battled on and made a life for you and Leigh[…] It's surprising how so small a frame could house so large a spirit – I know her faith meant a great deal to her.[7]

The Faithfull family tree[8] is full of army officers, Indian civil servants, missionaries and Anglican clergymen. Notable among the latter is the Rev. Francis Joseph Faithfull (1786–1854) who was tutor to the young James Gascoyne-Cecil, later the Marquess of Salisbury who lived at the great Hatfield House in Hertfordshire. Francis Joseph became rector of Hatfield and ran a boarding school there for a select group of aristocratic pupils. He was a staunch supporter of Sunday observance.[9] Lucy had a photo of his portrait amongst her papers. There are also eminent women in the family. Francis Joseph's niece was Emily Faithfull (1835–95), who deserves to be wider known. At a time when middle-class women were supposed to be confined to the domestic sphere, or, if employed, effectively limited to governessing, she championed wider employment opportunities and set up a publishing house for women in 1860. The Victoria Press in Coram Square, Bloomsbury, used only female compositors and Emily took a maternal interest in their welfare. Male print union opposition to this innovation was intense. Among Emily's productions was an early women's journal, *The Victoria Magazine*, which was published for eighteen years and charted the progress of the women's movement, promoting the cause of women in employment, among other issues. Her work was so successful that, in 1862, she was appointed "Printer and Publisher in Ordinary to Her Majesty". In his short biography of Emily, Eric Ratcliffe writes that in 1863:

> she read a paper to the Edinburgh conference of the
> Social Science Association, denouncing pit brow work
> as unsuitable labour for women. Her inexhaustive will in
> campaigning for more female employment had a cut-off
> point when she thought she discerned any mode of work
> which she regarded as degrading to womanhood.[10]

Later in life she undertook, and wrote about, three visits to
the United States where she visited publishing houses, met with
eminent contemporaries and travelled as far as Denver and New
Mexico.[11] Although Lucy never labelled herself a feminist, she
repeated many aspects of Emily's way of campaigning. They both
were tireless in their efforts in pursuing issues that were important
to them, both demonstrated concern for the welfare of people
with limited choices in life, and, notably, both developed skills
in addressing Social Science conferences: Lucy was a devoted
conference attender and keynote speaker.

One of Francis Joseph's granddaughters was another notable
unmarried Faithfull, Lilian, who, after a long and distinguished
academic career, became Vice-Principal of King's College London
(Ladies' Department) and then Principal of Cheltenham Ladies'
College in 1907. Lilian shared Emily's pioneering spirit, as she
writes in her autobiography:

> For those of us who began our working life in the
> 'eighties, and belonged to almost the first generation
> of professional women, there was the added difficulty
> of having no precedents[...] We had to devise our own
> machinery, to determine our policy, and to inspire
> others with confidence when we had little ourselves
> [...] We were aware that women were on their trial
> as administrators and we often had to plough a lonely
> furrow.[12]

Lucy could have echoed that last sentence about many aspects of
her work as the only social worker in the House of Lords.

Another female Faithfull who gained fame, or notoriety, in the 1960s, and about whom there is speculation as to whether she was a relative of Lucy's, is Marianne Faithfull, the pop singer. She is indeed related, but only very distantly. Lucy is known to have expressed concern about Marianne's drug use, but the connection between them is tenuous.

To return to Lucy's own story, at the end of the First World War, Bessie and the children moved from Newport to Boscombe, Hampshire to be near Sidney's parents, Charles and Sarah Faithfull. (Charles had been a Protestant missionary in Spain and Sidney, Lucy's father, had actually been born in Madrid.) There, Bessie made friends with a family called Peake who ran a boys' prep school in Kent. She took up the post of matron at this school in return for a free education for Leigh. The Peakes must have been delighted to employ a qualified nurse at that time of shortage of all kinds of staff.

At the end of the War, after having already endured huge changes during her short life, moving from one continent to another, from one house to another, and losing her father, little Lucy was sent away, at the age of only seven, to boarding school. This is how she remembers the experience: "The night before I went I remember having the most terrible nightmare, and when Mother actually left me there I looked over the banisters to see her go, and I froze. It was such a terrible experience."[13] "I couldn't eat, I couldn't talk, I couldn't move", she told Terry Philpot,[14] in a terrible foreshadowing of the "frozen watchfulness" that she later saw among emotionally neglected children. She decided at a young age to become a social worker, but always thought back to that traumatic separation:

> From the point of view of one's early childhood affecting one, when I had to remove a child from home it always hurt most terribly because I remembered that first night and first day at boarding school. You mustn't let your own feelings affect what you're doing in your professional life, but in fact they're almost bound to, and I really felt strongly that one should never move a child from home unless it was absolutely necessary.[15]

Although she does not mention it, the separation must have been all the more painful because of her knowledge that Leigh was still in close contact with their mother, as she was employed by his school, not hers.

The school was Bournemouth Girls' High School (which still exists but as Talbot Lodge School and occupying a new site to which it moved soon after Lucy left). Of her girlhood there she writes:

> I wasn't really happy between seven and twelve [...] Children need to be by themselves sometimes, and at boarding school you never are. We weren't allowed in the dormitories during the day, and I used to creep up and creep under the bed, and it was an absolute relief to be by oneself just for a bit.[16]

My suspicion is that these early losses had a decisive influence on Lucy's future career. She had clearly had a loving and secure infancy in South Africa, during which the foundations for her stable personality had been laid down. However, the subsequent violent disruption of this happy life and the bereavements – real in the case of her father, and experienced in the case of her mother following her departure for boarding school and the resulting separation from her – gave her great empathy for children in trouble of all kinds. She remembered thinking, aged six, in the nursery of some friends, that things in her life were "not quite right". "I said to myself, all my life, when I'm grown-up, I'm going to work for children who are not happy."[17] "My childhood was never settled because we had no home. We would sleep in six different places during the year", she says. For ten years, Bessie and her children would go for Christmas holidays to the aunt and uncle in Newport; at Easter they would stay in 'rooms' in Boscombe to be near Sidney's parents, and, in the summer, visit friends in Kent. It was a not unhappy time, but Lucy always recognised that "there was something missing." Only after her grandmother died and bequeathed them some money did the family finally get a stable home, in Bournemouth. "It was lovely, it really was, to have one's own bedroom and not to have to move and to be able to stabilise."[18] Lucy was fifteen.

She eventually settled down at school, and felt well looked after. The school, she thought:

> was beautifully run, the staff were so devoted. It seemed to run on affection between staff and children. You couldn't have called it highly disciplined, and yet everything ran like clockwork, simply because the headmistress, Miss Broad, was so beloved. I was appalled, when I first took up social work, to see that some children were not treated as I had been treated. I loved school.

She joined in with boarding school fun such as having conversations in Morse code with torches after 'lights out', and made some enduring friendships. In old age she reminisces with her school friend Mollie, "I remember how fond Miss Webster was of you, [and] how you used to play Chopin in the common room". She reminds Mollie of Tora Robinson, who now lives in East Meon (the same village where her brother Leigh lived) and who was about to come to stay with her in Oxford, and Betty Edmonds "who used to be known as 'Pillow' because of her rounded figure." This group of friends met up quite regularly for very many years, often in Sussex because so many of them lived there.

The picture given of Lucy as she became more senior in the school is endearing. Her headmistress, in a reference written when Lucy was applying for child care training, said, "She was a girl of serious purpose and sympathetic outlook". In the boarding house where she was a prefect or monitor, "girls obeyed her willingly. She would always keep the girls in her dormitory in order, and happy.[19] I particularly like this last comment; Lucy always seemed to have the ability to make people she came into contact with happy.

Although the school was in the town, it had excellent playing fields. Lucy became captain of the tennis team. She did not see herself as academic, and confesses to not really working until she was a teenager, when she realised that she would need to apply herself in order to get into University. She managed four Higher School Certificates (the equivalent of modern A Levels). "I would have liked to go to Oxford, but Oxford hadn't got a social work training. And anyway I'm not sure that I would have been academically up to the standard".[20] She admired her English teacher, Miss Rowe, and it was at school that she discovered those "condition of England" novels by Dickens, Mrs Gaskell and Disraeli – "Dickens was my favourite from about twelve to fourteen" – and was "quite appalled" at some of the social conditions these authors described. By the age of fourteen, she had definitely decided to become a social worker. In addition to her own formative experiences, her grandparents and a favourite uncle, Edgar, had been missionaries, so good works were in her blood.

In what might be seen as an expected and conventional move for a daughter of the English professional classes, when she left school Lucy went to Paris at the invitation of another aunt and uncle. But, unlike other middle-class girls, she immediately started on her life project to work with children. She arranged to live in a settlement, La Résidence Sociale run by a Mademoiselle Bassot at 3, rue des Champs, in the Levallois-Perret district, a very poor part of Paris. Here, she worked in the nursery school where many of the toddlers were children of émigrés from the Russian Revolution. She was immediately flung in at the deep end. The second day that she was there, the head of the nursery fell ill and she was left to run the nursery without being able to speak a word of French, or indeed, Russian. "All I did was say to the children, 'faire ceci' and 'faire cela' […] They were absolutely enchanting, but I don't think they learned much, those children, during the fortnight that I looked after them",[21] she told Rebecca Abrams. She was obviously eminently suited to this work. A charming testimonial from La Résidence, written in 1932 in Franglais, declares, (the spelling and punctuation are original):

> Lucy Faithfull has been here for eight months. She helped
> with the kindergarter and gave full satisfaction for her
> manners and abilities she is remarquably gifted with

children, knows and understands them very well. She is very attentiv, faithfull [*sic*] and devoted to her duty.

Furthermore she did eventually learn some French.

In 1930, Lucy came back to England and went up to Birmingham University. Here she continued this pattern of combining study and social work by choosing to live in the Birmingham Settlement in Newtown,[22] an area of poverty and deprivation to the north of the city centre where people existed in dark and unsanitary back-to-back houses with limited daylight, poor ventilation and a heavily polluted atmosphere. Lucy said that the residents had "one wash-house to eight houses, and two loos to about sixteen houses."[23] One courtyard of this type of house, in Inge Street in central Birmingham, has been carefully restored by The National Trust. One of the houses is furnished as it might have been by a family visited by Lucy in the 1930s.

The Settlement movement had its origin in the 1880s in the context of "a groundswell of public opinion outraged by the plight of the poor".[24] In the 1840s, Disraeli's *Sybil, or the Two Nations* and Elizabeth Gaskell's *North and South* had brought these concerns into literature, and themselves created awareness of the squalor caused by industrialisation and the injustices of poverty. Educated people were increasingly becoming aware of the stark contrast between their own wealth and the poverty among the working classes.[25] The first Settlement in England, Toynbee Hall, was established in Whitechapel in 1884. By 1914, there were thirty-seven settlements in English cities. These became important centres of social work and helped to improve the health and welfare of people in their neighbourhoods. "Yet for all its good work and its significance, the settlement movement was based on social superiority".[26] Many of the 'settlers' themselves acknowledged this, and came to realize that they had a great deal to learn from their neighbours, who shared a close-knit community and a certain vitality and independence in the midst of deprivation.

From its very beginnings, social work has provided women, otherwise excluded from taking an active part in legal, social, economic and political aspects of life, with opportunities to develop their talents and energies for the good of society. In Birmingham, the story of the Women's Settlement, as it was initially called, is, as Glasby points out, "very much a gendered history, providing women with an opportunity to contribute to the local community and challenging existing gender roles".[27] In 1898, a group of ladies from the prosperous areas of Edgbaston, Harborne and Handsworth met to explore the possibility of founding a Settlement in Birmingham to be a centre for philanthropy, the study of industrial conditions and for systematic training for social workers.[28] The Settlement in Birmingham was set up with accommodation for five female residents, and the focus of the community work was work with women and children. From the outset there were very close links with the Quaker Cadbury family, and with the University of Birmingham. Many of the Executive Committee members were the wives of prominent academics. Successive Annual Reports of the Settlement set out its philanthropic aims "to promote the social, physical, intellectual and moral welfare of the people of the neighbourhood", and on the educational front, "to provide a centre for resident and non-resident workers for systematic study with reference to social work and industrial conditions," and to provide practical training for students taking the Social Study course at the University of Birmingham.[29]

Lucy was one of these resident workers. Birmingham was an outstanding local authority at that time, with a strong Quaker ethos and a deep commitment to serving the community. It was an exciting place to be and an exciting time to be there. She spent two years as a student volunteer at the Settlement, working in the many and various projects which were running at the time, doing the equivalent of the modern "practice placement" aspect of social work training, with the difference that Lucy and the other students lived full time in the community they were learning to serve. The people of Birmingham were kept fully informed of events at the Settlement by a *Birmingham Post* reporter signing him- or herself

Birmingham Settlement, Whit Monday 1930.

A.N. who enthusiastically wrote up every event of significance at
the Settlement: the Christmas parties, the AGMs, the summer trips,
and the talks.

Lucy must have attended a weekend conference at the Settlement
in April 1932. On the Friday night, the paper reports, Eleanor
Rathbone, then MP for the Combined English Universities, spoke
on "the place of the voluntary worker in the new social order".
In a strange foreshadowing of a comment that Lucy could herself
have made years later when she was in Parliament, Miss Rathbone
is quoted as saying:

> The House of Commons is full of elderly men who have
> achieved a certain amount of success in businesses from
> which they have retired, and of many young prosperous
> men who to their own surprise got in unexpectedly at
> the election. I sometimes listen with some amazement to
> those prosperous young men taking part in the debates in
> the House of Commons on housing and more frequently
> on unemployment. Many of them, I am afraid, have never
> really had any friendship with working class people in
> their lives.

She went on to suggest that every aspirant to political position should serve an apprenticeship in a settlement.[30]

Other talks and lectures were offered to the students on topics such as "the problem of women's wages", or "how to study social questions". Lucy writes:

> When I first went to the settlement, an extraordinary woman came to lecture, and she said, 'If you're going to be a good social worker, you work yourself out of existence. While you must be compassionate to those who are in need of money, and in need of a house, and in need of goods, your ultimate aim must be to help them to be completely independent, so that they can develop themselves and not be beholden to anyone'. We [still] haven't really worked this out properly: how on the one hand, you do not allow the vulnerable to sink below the poverty line; on the other hand you do your very best to help people to be independent'[31]

This dilemma stayed with Lucy all her life, I think, and played a part in her decision as to which party she should join when she was made a Life Peer. An extended article by the indefatigable A.N. with the engaging title, "Social Work Is Not So Dull As It Sounds" details the practical work done by students like Lucy at the Settlement:

> It includes office work (correspondence and the preparation and filing of records); visiting (in connection, for instance, with the work of the Citizens' Society, the Country Holiday Fund, after-care of school children [...]); factory welfare work; experience in a club or play centre; health work; and a little practical psychology. In addition to this practical work at least ten visits must be paid to institutions [...] Among the institutions visited by the social students are work-houses, cottage homes, the Children's Court, Home Office schools, hospitals and the Epileptic Colony. Meetings of the City Council are attended, housing improvements inspected and

employment exchanges visited. All students are required to write brief account of these visits of observation."[32]

This list gives a good idea of the types of institutions providing social services in the early 1930s. Many of these have now been superseded by less institutional services, but the kind of experience Lucy and her fellow students had would be recognisable to the modern social work student. We learn that students are not accepted at the Settlement under the age of 19, and that:

> Matriculation is not a necessary preliminary to the Social Study Diploma course, but a really good standard of education is required [...] Whole-time board at the Settlement costs 37s. 6d. a week, so for a session of 40 weeks the charge would be £75 [...]

The article goes on:

> Versatility and keenness are two essential qualities for the girl [sic] who wishes to take up social work as a career [...] she must be able to throw herself heart and soul into her job. Any form of social work will bring her so closely into contact with the drab side of life that without real enthusiasm she will never reach her goal. But if she has the right spirit, and regards it as a vocation as well as a career, the social worker finds her job one of the most interesting in the world."[33]

Lucy had the "right spirit" in spades.

At the University, she studied under the Professor of Commerce, P. Sargent Florence, and was awarded her Diploma in Social Policy and Social Work in 1933. She always felt it unjust that she had to take seven subjects including Psychology, Philosophy, Economics, and Public Health at University level, and cram it all into two years, but only come out with a Diploma rather than a degree. The fact that social work was not then seen as a degree subject itself tells us something of the status of the profession in the 1930s; it was still regarded just as an occupation for well-meaning women.

Consciousness of her lack of a proper academic degree remained with Lucy all her life.

The end of her time at the Settlement was marked by one of the annual dances put on for club members by the students. The *Birmingham Post* reporter was there again:

> Students ran up and down with lemonade. [They] made short speeches, well seasoned with jokes. They all said that their years at the Settlement [...]were among the happiest of their lives [...] Helpers ran to and fro, collecting up plates, moving chairs, thrusting papers and crusts through the hatch, folding sweeping and lifting away trestles. Suddenly the centre was empty, the chairs were lined round the sides and the band, perspiring, with much show of large handkerchiefs, had appeared on the platform [...] the students danced continually. Many girls and a shy youth or two from the clubs they organized came and asked them for dances.

Waxing poetic, the journalist continues:

> I went out from the crowded bright hall into the street, it had been raining [...] the entrances to the courts were dark and full of puddles, and above black chimneys poured smuts against a black sky. Looking back at the Settlement one could see the lines of lighted windows [...] it stood there as a refuge from the squalor of the streets.[34]

After she finished her training, Lucy became a member of staff at the Settlement, first as a club leader and then as sub-warden. She says of her work there:

> The unemployment in those days was appalling. Anyone who was in trouble would come and ask for help. We ran clubs and took them [...] to plays, arranged games for them, arranged country holidays for them. We used to take the children away for weekends in the country and in the summer we used to take them for a fortnight to a little

village called Powick where we had the village hall. We ran clubs for every age – for little ones, for the school-children, for the young men and women, and we ran a dance every other Saturday night for the adolescents. Then there was the mothers' club and the fathers' club. We had sixty volunteers and some of them would come and teach art, and […] dressmaking, and […] teach the boys metalwork. In any one week, there were about four or five hundred [people] coming to clubs. It was morning noon and night. […] it was an exciting time. There were really exciting people, they were stimulating, there were ideas. My mother came to stay and she thought it was the most terrible place and she never came again, but I simply loved it.

I do empathise with Lucy in her experience of her mother's ambivalence about her choice of life and career. When I decided to become a social worker in 1973, I remember my otherwise sweet and compassionate mother questioning why I wanted to work with "all those smelly people". Lucy continues:

On a Monday morning, all the students had to collect money for the Birmingham Provident Fund. You had a bag and you visited every house in your district and you tried to persuade people to pay into the Provident Bank. They would pay in twopence, threepence, fivepence, and you would mark it up on their card, and mark it in your book. I always visited Brearly Street, which was one of the worst streets. We always went alone, and we always carried these bags of money. Everyone knew that we'd got a bag of money and never at any time was any one of us attacked. Yet it was such a bad district that the police used to go about in threes! It was extraordinary.[35]

Provident collecting had been a Settlement initiative to combat the financial and material deprivation in the area. The few pence a week that people saved in the Provident scheme was the only chance they had to put aside small sums to tide them over when

Lucy in the doorway of a back-to-back.

times got even tougher. The scheme also provided regular contact, "a valuable means of establishing friendly relationships" with local people, an easy and natural way of entering into touch [...] [and] getting to know their needs".[36]

In the mid-thirties, in an effort to clear the slums around the Settlement, a new housing estate was built on compulsorily purchased land on the outskirts of Birmingham at Kingstanding, and families began to be decanted miles away from their relatives and friends and their work. This seriously alarmed Lucy. Her anxiety about separation and disruption, with its roots perhaps in her own experiences, shows through:

> In those days there were no social facilities. There wasn't a library, there wasn't a swimming centre, there weren't churches, there weren't many shops; there were just houses and houses and houses. We were so upset about it that we used to run clubs in the evening in a school for them in order that they would feel connected with the place from which they had been moved.[37]

She would have preferred the slums to be replaced with new

houses in the same area so that people could be kept in their own community.

Lucy continued her work in Newtown and Kingstanding all through her early twenties.

Notes:

[1] All documents referred to are, unless otherwise attributed, in the archive at St Hilda's College, Oxford.
[2] Rebecca Abrams, *Woman in a Man's World*, (London: Methuen, 1993) p. 21.
[3] The pension, from the Office of the High Commission for the Union of South Africa, Trafalgar Square, was in fact for £257/16, "until remarriage".
[4] Rebecca Abrams, *The Birmingham Post*, p. 22.
[5] Rebecca Abrams, *Lucy Faithfull*. Tape transcription. British Library National Sound Archive. National Life Story collection. Ref. No. C408/013, 1989/1990.
[6] Philip Graham, "Personal Profile", *Child Psychiatry and Psychology Review*, 1 February 1996.
[7] Letter, "A" to Lucy Faithfull, (hereafter LF), 12 January 1962.
[8] The Faithfull family tree is comprehensively documented by a cousin of Lucy's, Brian Faithfull, who lives in Australia.
[9] Eric Ratcliffe, *The Caxton of her Age. The Career and Family Background of Emily Faithfull (1835– 95)*, (Upton-upon-Severn: Images, 1994), pp. 69–71.
[10] Ratcliffe, 1994, p. 38.
[11] Emily Faithfull, *Three Visits to America*, (Edinburgh: David Douglas, 1884).
[12] Lilian Faithfull, *In the House of My Pilgrimage*, (London: Chatto & Windus, 1924) quoted in Ratcliffe, 1994, p. 79.
[13] Abrams, *Woman in a Man's World*, p. 22.
[14] Terry Philpot, "Profile: Faithfull in her Fashion", *Community Care*, (20–27 December 1990), 16.
[15] Abrams, *Woman in a Man's World*, p. 23.
[16] Ibid, p. 23.
[17] Ibid, p. 25.
[18] Ibid, p. 24.
[19] Reference, 26 February 1936.
[20] Abrams, Tape transcription.
[21] Abrams, Tape transcription.

22 The Settlement is still at its original address, 318 Summer Lane.
23 Abrams, *Woman in a Man's World*, p. 26.
24 Jon Glasby, *Poverty and Opportunity: 100 Years of the Birmingham Settlement*, (Studley: Brewin Books, 1999) p. 9.
25 In 1883, Samuel Barnett, vicar of St Jude's in Whitechapel, one of the most notorious slums in London, gave a lecture at Oxford in which he made the proposal that a colony of educated men could live among the poor in a deprived area of a large city. They could educate them, learn from them, socialise with them and promote social reform.
26 Dr Carl Chinn in *Foreword* to Glasby, p. vii.
27 Glasby, p. 17.
28 The origins of the Birmingham Settlement are described in detail by Joyce Rimmer, in *Troubles Shared: The Story of a Settlement 1899–1979* (Birmingham: Phlogiston Publishing, 1980).
29 Annual Report, Birmingham Settlement, 1931.
30 *The Birmingham Post,* Saturday 29 April 1932.
31 Abrams, *Woman in a Man's World*, p. 24.
32 *The Birmingham Post*, 13 February 1932.
33 Ibid.
34 *The Birmingham Post,* 28 August 1933.
35 Abrams, *Woman in a Man's World*, pp. 26–27.
36 Annual Reports, Birmingham Settlement, 1901 and 1907.
37 Abrams, *Woman in a Man's World,* p. 26.

CHAPTER TWO

EVACUATION

In 1935, after Lucy had been at the Birmingham Settlement for five years, her mother and brother decided to move to London, to a modern house in Hampstead Garden Suburb, 9 Howard Walk. She was ready for a break, and came to join them. She also decided that she needed further training and applied to the British Officers' Fund for a grant for six months' training with the Charity Organisation Society.[38] This was specialist family casework training, and it was on the basis of having completed this course that, much later, in 1969, Lucy was awarded a Certificate as a qualified child care officer by the then Central Training Council in Child Care. Her fiercely independent mother disapproved of this grant application, saying Lucy had "lost her pride".[39]

For the next three years, she worked for the then London County Council (LCC), as the "Assistant child care organiser" in Bermondsey and Rotherhithe. The LCC had set up school welfare services in the early years of the century as a result of education legislation. The concern was primarily to meet children's material needs – hungry, tired and cold children cannot learn – and also to refer them to health, and later, psychiatric and psychological services. By the 1930s, London was divided into different Regions for purposes of education administration. Southwark and Bermondsey constituted District X. The senior official responsible for these Regions at County Hall was a Miss Marriott.

Assistant Organisers had to be professionally trained and have a wide knowledge of national and local social policy. Their work was overseen by local Child Care Committees. They were expected to recruit a body of volunteers to visit a group of individual schools, frequently and regularly, in order to address any child welfare issues of concern to the teachers that week. The expectations by the LCC of these paid organisers was that they should:

> keep themselves *au courant* with developing social legislation and the scope and functions of the innumerable voluntary societies, devoting themselves to specific forms of aid, training the voluntary worker by putting such information at her disposal, and to be available to give general advice.[40]

Lucy told Abrams about her work in this role:

> Rotherhithe was a most exciting place: the East End people were so full of life and vitality and humour that one enjoyed visiting the dockers. The care committee organiser was responsible for about twenty-six London schools; if the school felt that a child needed clothes (and some of them did), or needed food (and many of them did), or that there was something unhappy about the child, or something unhappy about the home, one of our volunteers [would] go and visit the home – or if there wasn't a volunteer you did it. You provided a link between the school and the home. I ran a team of voluntary workers.[41]

In Bermondsey, in Lucy's time, the Care Committee had various sub-committees. One that I imagine Lucy was closely connected with was the 'Outfits' sub-committee. This met regularly to approve grants to needy families, presumably referred by the schools. On Thursday 4th May 1939, for example, little Lydia Brown of Midway Place School was awarded 1s. 8 3/4d. for a vest and plimsolls, and Charles Williams of Albion Street School got the princely sum of 10s. 0d. for "boots, plimsolls and trousers".[42] The provision of boots for children seems to have been a high welfare priority of the time. This was a time of the Depression, after all, with high unemployment and widespread family poverty.

Lucy refers to "unhappy children". The 'Problem Cases Conferences' met in the regions to discuss and review individual cases of children who were thought to have learning or behaviour difficulties. Some children were referred for an ESN ('Educationally Sub-Normal') assessment, others were sent to residential establishments for 'maladjusted' children or to special facilities for deaf or hard-of-hearing children. As Lucy mentions, large numbers of children were referred to Child Guidance:

> If the school thought there was something, if the child was disturbed, you would arrange for the child to go to the Child Guidance Clinic. If there was something physically wrong with the child you would arrange, through the parents, for the child to go to […] Moorfields Hospital for instance if it was eyes, or Great Ormond Street. And I had a great deal to do with the Maudsley Hospital, because they had a very good Child Guidance Clinic.

The volunteers for whom she was responsible, Lucy explained, were well-off women from prosperous parts of town. Married women did not go out to work in those days and this kind of charity work was something they were able to do. Lucy pointed out, "I don't expect it would work now, but it did then: the social structure of England was different then, the East Enders were not resentful of the West Enders and the West Enders had a tremendous sense of service".

Lucy was not well paid. The salary for Assistant Child Care Officers in 1936 was £200 − £250, and had been unchanged since 1930. A memo from a Miss Nussey makes a plea for the salary offered to be more "commensurate with qualifications and experience", and, in the process, reveals the pressure for social work to become more of a profession:

> In most fields of employment coming under the title of

'Social Work' salaries are notoriously low. In the past, this type of work was largely undertaken by people with private means who could afford to work for a minimal salary, and many branches of social work are still organised by charitable societies who feel it incumbent on them to keep their administrative expenses, including the salaries of their workers, at the lowest possible level. It is not to the Council's credit that it should take advantage of these factors to exploit those of its employees who are engaged in administering its 'social work' activities.[43]

The role of the Child Care Organiser (or 'School Care Organiser' as others employed later in a similar role called it) and the Care Committees persisted until the early 1970s when the service in London was combined with the Education Welfare Service (which had been established in the late nineteenth century with a primary focus on school attendance).[4] This experience in the front line of child poverty in the education system must have stood her in good stead much later in life during her time at the House of Lords when she worked on successive Education Bills.

Lucy was, by now, a slim, petite and attractive twenty-five-year-old woman with a responsible job. Why was she not married? Various people have suggested to me that there was an important 'someone' who was later killed in the War, but I have found no evidence of such a person. The fact that it was, at that time, unheard of for a middle-class married woman to enter or remain in employment (as opposed to voluntary work) may begin to explain why she, with her tremendous talent for human relationships, did not marry. Once a woman employed, say, as a teacher, a civil servant, or indeed a social worker, married, she was forced to resign. Lucy had, I think, a very strong sense of vocation and a determination to improve the lot of those less fortunate than herself, especially children, and would not contemplate giving up the chance of carrying on this work for the sake of domestic tranquillity, the security of male support, (or even, perhaps, sexual fulfilment) and motherhood. Lucy herself later offered another, much sadder, explanation to Rebecca Abrams:

> I think really at the back of my mind, when I was young
> I really thought that I wouldn't make a good wife and
> mother simply because I hadn't had the background. Now
> that was not very explicit but I think it was implicit.[45]

Because she did not grow up in a home with a mother taking
care of the children and a father working, she had no model of
that kind of life. She was, as the song goes, "nobody's wife".[46] Her
overall sense of regret is palpable in her next sentence, "From a
career point of view one might have done well, but one may not
have done well perhaps in all spheres of life." People to whom I
have spoken who knew Lucy often speculate that she sublimated
her own maternal instincts into her work with children.

She was not short of male admirers, though. Attached to a
note from 'Harry' wishing her Happy New Year for 1960 is this
suggestive limerick:

> I knew a young woman called Lucy
> Whose shape one can only call juicy.
> She said 'It appears
> That I give men ideas
> I wish I weren't quite so seducy'!

Amongst her later papers I found letters from two men who
corresponded with her in loving tones that seem to go beyond
mere friendship. One was Hugh Richards, whose address in 1979
was 4 Mitre Court Chambers, EC4, suggesting he was a lawyer. He
writes, "Seeing you reminds me of such great happiness so long
ago that one feels one will never recapture and will never equal.
How good you were for me then – I am eternally grateful."[47]
That sounds to me like love! Years later, when Lucy was made
a peer, Hugh proposed that he and "kid brother" Leigh jointly
arrange a celebration party for her.[48] Another admirer was Bill
Elliott, a widower, who lived in Farthinghoe, Northamptonshire,
and who sent Lucy lover-like letters, one of which also asked for
Lucy's help in writing a sermon.[49] (He had got a First in Classics at

Queen's College, Cambridge, and he served for thrty-one years in a variety of posts in the Inspectorate of Schools, HMI, becoming Chief Inspector from 1967 to 1972.[50] Lucy always had a gift for friendship. One of her women friends from this period in her life was an LCC colleague, Beryl Hughes, and she and her husband, Bill (later Principal of Ruskin College, Oxford) became life-long friends.

Late in 1938, Lucy moved, still as an LCC care committee organiser, to the as yet un-gentrified Islington, where poverty and crime were acute problems. "You'd have these lovely houses, with about eight families living in one house, with perhaps two rooms per family." She worked at Canonbury Child Guidance Clinic and her experiences there intensified still further her interest in the psychological and emotional needs of children. At the time when Lucy did her initial training at Birmingham and later with the Charity Organisation Society, social work education was informed largely by psychoanalytical insights derived from the work of Freud and Melanie Klein. Social work holds the 'middle ground' between the individual's inner world and the environment in which he/she lives. Without an understanding of the inner world, and the early experiences that have formed the personality, any practical steps that social workers take to help the person will be less effective. This perspective became deeply unfashionable in the early 1960s with the growth of the influence of academic Sociology, and the insistence that the main task of social work was the relief of poverty.[51] But back in the late 1930s, the psychodynamic perspective held sway, and Lucy was keen to be part of it. She decided she wanted to do yet more training, to become a psychiatric social worker, but the outbreak of War in 1939 prevented this and took her in another direction.

As the prospect of another war with Germany became imminent, authorities in urban and industrial areas feared that their populations would be bombarded from the air. In 1938, the LCC, under its energetic leader, Herbert Morrison, decided that evacuation of children from the danger zones in central London would be necessary, but that it would be voluntary; families could decide to register their children for evacuation, or to keep them at home. Receiving areas, however, would be compelled to take the evacuees into their homes.

Richard Titmuss, in his official history of the social aspects of the War,[52] points out that the Government was asking a great deal of the British people. "It was asking parents to send their children for an indefinite period to an unknown destination, there to be committed to the care of strangers." "Much depended on the efficiency of local preparations in each evacuation area and particularly on the quality of the relationship between those responsible for preparatory work – from councillors to teachers – and the parents." "The art of democratic persuasion, of making people feel confidence in the government's plans, had to be practised at the local – as well as national – level." Lucy was one of these local organisers. Registration was carried out in schools, and in Islington parents were told that they could put any questions to Miss Lucy Faithfull in her office in Pentonville Road, but she was unable to tell anxious parents where their children were going.[53]

The careful organisation of the entraining arrangements – particularly in London – was aided by the exercises and rehearsals carried out earlier in the summer. Once the evacuation began, on September 1st 1939, the children were "guided by an array of banners, armlets and other devices, and marshalled by an army of teachers and voluntary helpers". Over 40,000 of these helpers accompanied the children and were billeted in the reception areas. Despite these careful plans, in the event there was considerable chaos at the railway stations. Less than half of the expected numbers of children and mothers turned up, which led to extensive changes in train schedules and destinations. This meant, in many receiving areas, the arrival of different categories of evacuees than those planned for. For example, baffled householders were suddenly faced with billeting groups of seventeen-year-old schoolboys instead of the mothers with young children they had been led to expect. Lucy describes her role:

Evacuees

I was delegated to take parties of children, and also
mothers, out into the country. The children were all wildly
excited, because in those days people didn't travel as they
travel now, and it was a tremendous excitement for these
children going out, with their little gas masks bumping
on their back, and their little suitcases. Then, as the time
came for the train to go off, a kind of silence fell, and
the women would weep, and the children began to be
apprehensive, so that when the train pulled out there was
this tremendous silence among the children, a terrible
apprehensiveness at what was going to happen.[54]

The first group of mothers and children she accompanied
were en route to Marlborough. She told an interviewer for a
BBC television programme "*Where were you on the day War broke
out?*"[55] that she was terrified that a baby might be born during the
journey. Although she was equipped with a 'little kit', she would
have no idea what to do. Sure enough, a heavily pregnant woman
declared that her baby was coming, but calmed Lucy by assuring

her, "Don't worry ducks, I've had three already". The fourth was born soon after they reached their destination. Another trip was to Oxford, and after ensuring that all the children were safely billeted, and at a late hour, Lucy had nowhere to sleep herself. She was taken in by a kindly woman, who, as Lucy had no night clothes, offered her as a nightdress the burial gown which she had been carefully saving for her own funeral.

Once the children arrived at their rural destination, they were usually herded into village halls where the local prospective foster mothers were assembled to select their boarders. "The selection process seemed designed to emphasise the power of the foster parents and the powerlessness of the evacuees", writes Bob Holman. There would always be a child or small group left till last, or not chosen at all. Lucy always felt pain on their behalf, "I used to go up to that child and say, 'you're so important that you are the last to be chosen.' What the child made of that I can't say".[56]

There is a mass of archival material relating to plans for evacuation, mainly concerning administrative arrangements and emergency provision. One draft circular of 1939 does anticipate the kind of social and inter-personal problems that would arise, but it was thought at that time that these problems could be adequately dealt with by existing local authorities and 'voluntary effort'.[57] This was to prove a drastically unrealistic assessment.

The Government had anticipated a massive bombing campaign from the moment War was declared. Titmuss points out that the physical safety of mothers and children from all-out, intensive and prolonged air bombardment by day and night was the first and dominant concern. Much less thought was given to the emotional effects of sudden and drastic separation. "Inevitably, the effect on the sensitive mechanism of the child's mind took second place". He adds that: "from the first day of September 1939 evacuation ceased to be a problem of administrative planning. It became instead a multitude of problems in human relationships."[58]

This was the so-called "phoney war"; no bombs fell. People who could bear the splitting up of their families if it was to save lives could not sustain this separation in the absence of real

　　　　　　　　　　　　Lucy Faithfull: mother to hundreds

and immediate danger, and, to the Government's consternation, children and families began to trickle back to the designated danger zones. Some stations saw parties of children arriving on one platform, with groups of mothers and children on the opposite platform waiting for the train back to town. But then in September 1940 came the Blitz, which prompted a second wave of evacuation, and this time it was better organised. Lucy told Abrams:

> A remarkable woman called Miss Geraldine Aves, who worked at County Hall and who was the Chief Welfare Officer, asked me if I would go into the country and act as a Regional Welfare Officer advising local authorities on the welfare and well-being of the evacuees in the area of Derbyshire and [...] Leicestershire. There were Regional Officers such as myself in every area of England.

In fact, Geraldine Aves was seconded to the Ministry of Health, and Lucy was one of four hand-picked officers from the London County Council who were seconded to central government. Around November 1940, this group was supplemented by sixteen further appointments. Lucy went to Region 3, North Midland, reporting to the Senior Regional Officer, E.S. Hill. The office was based in Nottingham, and her National Insurance book shows her living at 1 Alpha Terrace, North Sherwood Road, Nottingham. The house still exists today and is one of a row of tall Victorian houses to the North of the city centre, set at right angles to the main road with windows looking over a dusty little park and the smoky city.

Lucy told Bob Holman of an occasion when she took a group of evacuee children for their first walk in the country. One child, seeing cows for the first time in his life, asked her, "Miss, whatever are those horses with handlebars?"

An astonishing six million people were moved out of the urban areas of Britain in the early years of the War. It is well known that the evacuation of children from deprived inner-city areas caused a shock to middle-class rural families suddenly confronted with ill-clad, under-fed, and sometimes verminous children. Titmuss wrote of the "miles of rubber sheeting that had to be found and issued to stem the tide of bedwetting that swept the reception areas, and the special residential facilities that had to be developed to house the 'unbilletable'".[59] These "unbilletable" children were those with physical or mental handicaps or with infectious conditions or intractable behaviour problems; hostels were established to provide special care for them. Many of the children brought psychological problems with them, and more developed difficulties when faced with long periods of separation from, and sometimes the distant death of, their parents. Foster parents, as they were often called even then, found many of these children destructive and defiant. The Billeting Officer in one area painted a 'rather black picture' of uncontrollable boys, the place of honour being held by two young chaps who had destroyed rose trees to make bows and arrows.[60] My goodness.

More severe difficulties were presented by mothers who were evacuated with their pre-school children. Host families were in culture shock. The differences between guest and hosts are picturesquely, if stereotypically, described by Geoffrey Shakespeare MP in his report of 1941:

> The London woman is gregarious. The busy multitudes, the crowded streets and shops, the cinemas and similar diversions form the background of her life. She is not overburdened with domesticity. She has a partiality for tinned foods and readily resorts to the fish and chip stall. The life of her sister in the country parish or provincial town is more centred on her home [...] Outside her home the social activities of the Churches and the Women's Institute occupy her leisure hours.[61]

Titmuss makes the telling point that practically all of the mothers who were sent to reception areas in the early years of the War had spent some part of their childhood and youth during the First World War of 1914–18, and for many it had "not been well spent". Not only had medical and education services been diverted away from child welfare during that period, but also, at a critical period of their lives, children had missed their fathers, and often mothers too. "How many lives were harmed in childhood and adolescence by the death or disablement of fathers?" he asks. War has devastating long-term, hidden consequences. He also points out that two million people had evacuated privately prior to September 1939, making their own arrangements to stay with family or friends away from danger, so that the families who took part in the government scheme were those without the resources to organise their own evacuation; in other words, the poor or what would now be called "socially excluded" groups of people.

Meanwhile, up in the Midlands, Lucy was finding herself in the middle of a revolt in Derbyshire, in an area that had received a large group of children from Manchester.[62] Lucy told Bob Holman:

> [The children] were really difficult and rough. I don't mean that they were unpleasant, they were enchanting, but their habits were appalling. The people of Derbyshire experienced them doing their jobbies on the floor in the sitting rooms. The women approached the Dowager Duchess of Derbyshire [sic][63] who told the Ministry of Health, on behalf of the people, that they refused to have the children in their homes.[64]

She continues the story:

> The town clerk of Derby made the town hall available and notices were sent out. The Duchess mustered all her friends from the county houses, the billeting officers got the foster parents and the town hall was full. The Duchess was in the chair and said, 'Miss Faithfull, we want the Government to know that we think these children should be kept in camps and not in private houses where they disrupt lives and damage furniture with their habits'. Several people spoke from the floor and platform and finally I was expected to speak. I said that I appreciated their difficulties but that war was hard. I went on, 'I want to ask you one question: if we put all the children under

canvas or in a hall or all together elsewhere and it was bombed and all the children were killed, would you really feel happy?' There was a silence and finally one woman got up and said, 'I can't possibly face such a situation. I'll take children.' From that moment we had no trouble.[65]

In later life, Lucy's ability to influence the opinion of Duchesses was to become an important skill in her work in the House of Lords.

An issue that caused particular difficulty was the question of billeting allowances. The system for recouping from parents left behind in the evacuation areas the cost of maintenance of their children in the country was complicated and time-consuming. There was constant pressure from better-off foster parents for higher rates. They often wanted to give their evacuated children the same standard of food, education and recreation that they gave their own children, and found the allowance insufficient for this. In April 1940, one Regional Officer summed up a series of gloomy reports: "The plain fact is that the reception areas are not far short of open revolt".[66]

One result of these difficulties was that receiving authorities recruited a veritable army of volunteer women child care visitors who were expected to see the families once a month and help the carers cope with problems. It was one of the tasks of the regional welfare officers such as Lucy to advise and support these visitors.

The part played by regional welfare officers in the evacuation story is little known though it was much valued at the time. A Ministry of Health Circular[67] describes the qualifications and experience of social work needed by welfare officers, and gives a good idea of the kind of things Lucy was doing during the War years. She was to stimulate, advise and give practical assistance to local authorities in the development of welfare provision for evacuees and people made homeless by bombing. She was expected to advocate the pooling of services, spread knowledge of better standards, assist with the recruitment of welfare staff, inspect hostels and other institutions, and deal with individual needs and difficulties. A thorough, almost encyclopaedic, knowledge of all the health and social services in an area well beyond the confines of a single authority was, therefore, an essential part of the equipment of a good welfare officer.

Geoffrey Shakespeare's report found that "Welfare Officers appointed to the Regional Staffs of the Ministry of Health have proved their worth", and recommends the appointment of more of these women who understand "the psychology of London mothers" and have the knowledge of social legislation that was necessary if they were to give "skilled advice".[68]

Geraldine Aves, the Chief Welfare Officer whom Lucy so much admired, wrote a comprehensive (although she called it 'Preliminary') report[69] in May 1941 for the Minister of Health on the development of welfare work. She had personally visited six of the Regions, perhaps including the Midlands. She points out that "all these officers have academic qualifications as professional social workers and/or considerable experience of general social work". The report sets out the formidable range of tasks expected of, and carried out by, Lucy and her fellow Welfare Officers:

> The development of social centres for evacuated women and such adjuncts as laundry, nursery, occupational recreational and feeding facilities; hostels of various types including communal billets; setting up of Welfare committees and arrangements for the supervision of unaccompanied children in billets; promoting the appointment of suitable Welfare workers by County and local authorities; the encouragement of out-of-school activities; the operation of clothing schemes and methods of dealing with individual problems, such as the encouragement of Child Guidance facilities, skilled billeting for misfits, and so on.
>
> The process followed in dealing with this variety of subjects is always the same, viz. the stimulating of local authorities to take appropriate action, helping to ascertain

and harness available voluntary effort, keeping in touch with representatives of other Government Departments, and helping to train and advise Social Workers appointed by local authorities. This involves great mobility in view of the large area covered and the importance of personal contacts with the many local authorities and individuals concerned, many of whom have to be nursed gently into willingness to undertake more for the benefit of evacuated persons and many of whom, though full of goodwill, are frequently ignorant of the framework of social services and amenities which the displaced City dweller requires or of the possible solutions of the many social problems which evacuation as brought in its train.

The skills that Lucy and the other Welfare Officers demonstrated in carrying out these multifarious and sensitive tasks are typical of Social Work. Then as now, they are carried out inconspicuously, and are only noticed by their absence. Air crews won the Battle of Britain, fire-fighters put out fires, rescue workers dug out the injured from the rubble, but, as Titmuss points out:

> The worker in the rest centre, billet or information office reached no such operational finality. He or she could diminish, but never remove, the sufferings of homeless people and the fears of evacuated children.[70]

Lucy and her colleagues were carrying out an absolutely essential and highly skilled role, and one that is, even now, unsung and uncelebrated.

Geraldine Aves reports that Welfare Officers had to work in often "absurdly inadequate" accommodation, in crowded rooms where interviews are impossible; they had sometimes to share a "deal table" and had nowhere to keep papers. She is impressed with the dedication of the officers, writing:

> I have not yet met any seconded Welfare Officer who thought it proper to contemplate taking the full leave to which she is entitled. On the other hand I should not feel

Lucy Faithfull: mother to hundreds

justified, for reasons of health and efficiency, in advising any Welfare Officer to whittle her leave down to one week, nor do I think it reasonable to expect the other Welfare Officers to limit themselves to so meagre a break.

She concludes that she is "well impressed" by the way in which these officers are tackling their many tasks.

Of course, accommodation was not the only need of evacuated mothers and children. The Inspector for Education in Hertfordshire painted a gloomy picture of the life of evacuees at the end of 1939:

Hostesses do not as a rule consider the payment by the Government of 5s a week for the mother and 3s for the child as covering more than the bare bedroom accommodation and the result was that the evacuees found themselves practically homeless during the day, with no facilities for bathing the children, for washing or ironing the clothes, or even for providing them with a properly cooked meal. In many cases they were expected to do these things in the bedroom [...] The children themselves have very little done for them. There are a few toys for which they can scramble and fight. There is no peace or confidence here for the children to build upon. They are out-of-hand, nervous and fretful, lacking sleep, proper nourishing food, regular milk and medical attention, and they are for the most part under-clothed. There is no quiet for them nor for their mothers, and it is agreed [...] that there is a most urgent need for the opening of places of organised assembly and self-respecting occupation for them if they are to remain or become useful members of society.[71]

Children needed somewhere to play, and mothers needed respite. Eventually, the Government responded to calls from such people as Lady Allen of Hurtwood and encouraged local authorities to set up day care centres. Lucy tried to set up some in the Midlands, but it was not all plain sailing:

> We ran into difficulties because we could not subscribe
> to the high standards demanded by the doctors and
> educationalists for the nurseries. I set up several groups,
> they were more like today's playgroups, but the doctors
> and educationalists closed some of them, not realising
> what it meant to the women to have one or two hours
> free. An enormous number of professional women had
> gone into the forces so we could not get qualified staff.[72]

Some Medical Officers of Health considered that women
should stay at home with their children, a belief that might have
lain behind this otherwise admirable insistence on high standards.
Lucy would have shared this view, and she did not attempt to
set up full-time day nurseries. A few hours spent at a playgroup
would be another matter, though, and eventually, as Holman
reports, the government overcame the staffing difficulties and by
1944, thousands of children were in some form of nursery group.
The War years saw a massive growth in day care provision. In fact,
the crisis of War and the evacuation stimulated many creative
initiatives in work with children.

While Lucy was in the Midlands, her later friend and
contemporary Clare Britton (later to marry and form an influential
partnership with the psychoanalyst Donald Winnicott), was doing
similar work in Oxfordshire. Her biographer, Joel Kanter,[73] writing
about Clare, could just as well be describing Lucy:

> [Her] work with evacuated children was the defining
> experience of her life … her talents as a social worker
> emerged at a time when Britain was undergoing
> a dramatic change in its child welfare policies and
> programmes. The work of Clare and her colleagues
> established precedents that altered the course of children's
> services for the half-century.

After Lucy had spent three years trouble-shooting in the
Midlands, she was sent to Plymouth, which had recently been

Lucy Faithfull: mother to hundreds

heavily bombed, to act as regional welfare officer for Devon and Cornwall. She was given a car, and stayed in the West Country for the rest of the War. An uncharacteristically florid journal entry she made in December 1945 gives a hint of her heightened state of mind at this time in her life. She writes in the dead of night, reflecting on her day:

> It has just struck one, first by the Customs House clock which is down on the quayside by the Barbican. It has a dull, metallic, inexorable clang, it seems to take for granted that time passes. A few seconds later St Andrew's clock has chimed [...] its notes linger on, are caught by the wind and borne away; it seems to regret the passing hour. It is dark, the wind is rasping, whistling and tearing up the streets and round the houses. Doors rattle and a sign swings on its hinges, creaks, whines. In how many houses are there people awake and wondering at this dark wild hour? What has passed today?

> This morning the office cat took possession of my lap while I was working at my desk, and as if it had no bones in its body it drooped itself across my knees; letters had to be written and the phone answered so that it should not be disturbed.[74]

She goes on to describe the rest of her day, in a tone of depression and weariness. She had lunch with Nora, who is good-looking but unhappy. Lucy thinks she should be married, but reflects that women living through this War "are robbed by circumstances of their vitality, burn with a dull light, life passes them by", and become unattractive to men. Is she talking about herself?

> Later with Sue we fetched five casefuls [sic] of crockery and bore them to her school. Why is it that elementary schools throughout this kingdom smell the same – they all have a dull, humourless smell of human sweat and disinfectant?

At 6 o'clock I fetched John Lloyd and took him to the
station in the car. The ten-minute ride was unsatisfactory
as one wanted it to last much longer and hear his wit and
humour.

[Then I] visited a carpenter and his wife living in a dark
and dreary street behind the Royal Naval Barracks which
so close resembles a prison worse than Dartmoor. The
carpenter, lately out of the navy, discoursed with heat and
bitterness on the domestic and foreign affairs of England,
all based on personal motives. He cannot get his own
property back and must live in one room because his
tenants in their turn cannot find accommodation.[75]

She had supper with Jack who, she thinks, is "ever at war with
himself". He enjoys people, but all the time is "craving to write
and leave something of lasting value behind him". Until he can
reconcile the two aspects of himself he will never be happy,
she writes. Bob Holman interviewed Lucy for his book on the
evacuation. She told him about her work in this period of her life
in some detail:

I only had one night of bombing in Plymouth but it was
a terrible night. I thought my last hours had come. I was
staying in the Settlement [again] and a bomb fell just up
the road so that the whole place was shaken and the lights
fell in. Devon and Cornwall already had a large number
of evacuee children from London but now children had
to be moved out of Plymouth. Then London had another
terrible night of bombing and yet more places had to be
found. I went to the clerk of the council in Truro and told
him the Ministry had asked me to find billets in Truro
for about 400 children [...] I told him the bombed out
children in London were waiting in schools. He agreed to
call a meeting of the Council that night and I went to it
and [...] they said, 'But we don't know you. We've never
met you before. We can't give you an answer straightaway'.

They told me to come back the next night and this time they agreed. I also had problems in Ilfracombe where people just refused to take any foster children. The children had arrived and were staying in schools looked after by teachers and volunteers. I had to live in Ilfracombe for three months and eventually, by visiting and persuasion got them to change their minds."[7]

I am impressed by the skills Lucy, then still in her early thirties, demonstrated in this unenviable job; her lobbying of the right people, her powers of persuasion, and, no doubt, her use of her personal charm, which she modestly does not mention, all stood her in good stead much later both in her professional life and in the House of Lords.

Children were not Lucy's only concern. She continues:

I was also responsible for a number of old people who were evacuated. We requisitioned a very prestigious hotel and used it for forty to fifty old people. A town clerk phoned me to say he had a terrible problem. The billeting officer could not find anywhere for an old lady, who was a lavatory cleaner in London, who was absolutely filthy, crawling. I rang up the matron at the hotel and said, 'You must take her but have a bath ready'. I picked up the old lady and told her she would have to have a bath. 'I've never had a bath', she said, 'And I'm not going to start now'. I stopped the car and told her that if she would not have a bath then I would leave her at the gate. So she agreed. When we arrived, matron whisked her upstairs to the bathroom. She was amazed to see her whip off a wig with the words, 'The young lady said I must wash from top to toe'. So she washed herself and her wig. She was in a room with a balcony. Suddenly we heard this terrible scream and rushed upstairs. She had hung her wig on the balcony to dry and a seagull had swooped and flown off with it. There she was as bald as a coot. I fetched my hat and put it on her. She looked rather nice. It took me six months to get the money out of the Ministry to replace her wig."[77]

Typical of Lucy is her detailed attention to people's needs. One can imagine the bureaucratic difficulties involved in getting a wig replaced. What budget category would that come under, one wonders? I think Lucy must have dined out on this amusing story for some years because in her archive I found a letter from Henry Maddock of Birmingham University recalling the episode, "I cannot pass the Idle Rocks Hotel in St Mawes without thinking of that wonderful story of the wig!"[78]

The hotel still exists. Its publicity tells us: "The Idle Rocks sits on the edge of the harbour wall in the quaint fishing village of St Mawes, on the tip of the Roseland Peninsular. The view from the hotel is the Cornish dream brought to life."

Both in Plymouth and in the fishing villages and coves along the South West coast, the Normandy invasion was being planned and rehearsed. Large areas were taken over by the military, with Slapton Sands and its hinterland, for example, being used to practise the assault on what was to be Utah beach. Because there were children billeted along the coast and in fishermen's houses, Lucy had a special permit to go to all the little seaside places where the general public were forbidden, and had a very clear idea about the date for the invasion. "One day the streets and the pubs would be full of the Navy, and then all of a sudden there was nobody about", she told Abrams.

While Lucy was charming town councillors and replacing wigs in the West Country, she heard of events of great import, at home and across the other side of the world. In July 1945, the wartime coalition government under Winston Churchill was defeated in the general election by Clement Attlee's Labour party. Herbert Morrison, ex-leader of the London County Council took his cabinet seat, and the programme of social reform that had been developed in the minds of politicians and civil servants during the war began to be implemented.

In August 1945, atomic bombs were dropped on Hiroshima and

Nagasaki, the war ended, and London saw huge demonstrations of joy in the streets on VJ (Victory over Japan) day.

The evacuation scheme ended, for all intents and purposes, by the end of March 1946. By then, there were only 5,200 unaccompanied children left in the reception areas. Lucy returned to her job in Islington. Social workers were much in demand to deal with some of the difficulties of adjustment arising in the homes of returning evacuees. The Ministry of Health advised local authorities to arrange for follow-up visits to be made to homes where children had returned. No doubt Lucy took up this task.

Abrams asked Lucy what she learned from her work as regional welfare officer. Lucy replied that the experience had influenced all the work she did subsequently.

> A lot of the evacuees were very well looked after physically, but emotionally [...] while some of them came to terms with their separation from their families, a lot of them didn't, although they managed to live life day by day. Now it made me realise really what families meant to children, even if they weren't good homes. And how much damage we did to children, taking children away from their homes.[79]

The whole process of evacuation prompted the beginnings of research in Britain into child development. It started with a concern for physical growth as an indicator, using the sometimes strange, to our ears, terms of the times. For example a Dr E.R. Bransby of the Ministry of Health carried out between 1941 and 1945 an "Anthropometric Investigation" into the height and weight of children evacuated from inner city schools to rural 'camp schools', comparing them with non-evacuated children. When Lucy got back to Islington after the War, returning to the LCC from her secondment to the Ministry of Health, she carried out some of her own research on behalf of the local authority to examine the effect of evacuation on children.

> We took several streets in Islington, and we visited all the families in those streets, so that they had the same

backgrounds, and we divided them into those where the children had been evacuated, and those that had stayed at home with their families, not going to school, sleeping in the underground with their parents, not having school milk. And we filled in all these forms from all these families, and […] we had a team of people analysing them, social worker, psychiatrist, psychologist, teacher, health visitor. And the outcome of that inquiry was that the children who had stayed with their parents were taller, were heavier, were emotionally better balanced, were psychologically at ease with themselves.[80]

Children who had been evacuated, they found, even when they had gone to very good foster homes, had a greater degree of emotional disturbance than those who had stayed with their families in the danger area, even though those children had often endured horrendous situations in shelters, witnessed death and destruction, and been short of food and medical attention. Lucy allows that evacuation may have saved many children's lives, but Holman believes she was always against evacuation. "Lucy Faithfull was involved in the evacuation from beginning to end. Looking back at it after fifty years, she was quite sure that it would have been better if the evacuation could have been avoided", he writes.[81] She told Abrams, "In my later life, as an inspector in the Home Office, as a children's officer in Oxford, as a Director of Social Services, I really always worked towards keeping children with their families where possible". This was undoubtedly related to her wartime experience of evacuation. She also consciously makes links with her own childhood experience. Her very next sentence is:

> I regretted very much not being at home; I regretted that I went to boarding school so young, and my brother went to boarding school even younger than me. I recognised that people who run children's homes and boarding schools have got much to offer, but in the final analysis it really is home and family which counts.[82]

Lucy's experience of early separation from both her parents and her brother, and her lack of a stable home must have given her empathy for those children who had been separated from their families by evacuation. At Kingstanding she had seen the damage caused by the disruption of stable neighbourhoods; her life as a child, a student, as a young social worker and as a wartime Regional Welfare Officer all served to strengthen her conviction that children need love, stability and to be with their own families almost at all costs.

From her work in Bermondsey and Islington, and especially in her work with evacuees in the War, Lucy Faithfull must have built up a valuable store of social work experience, from meeting the pressing needs of hundreds of children and families to accessing resources, organising and supporting volunteers, starting and maintaining projects of different kinds, negotiating with top officials of local authorities, and keeping abreast of ever-changing social policy. She must have carried out all these tasks with conspicuous flair and efficiency because she came to the notice of the Ministry of Health. That she had moved to the forefront of the child care field is demonstrated by the fact that, after the War, she was employed as an Inspector, no less, at the Children's Branch of the Home Office.

Notes:

[38] The COS had been set up to improve the standard of administering charity relief in London, emphasising the need for self help, and accompanying it with individual personal care. In the 20th century, the COS was associated with the development of social casework in Britain. The housing reformer and founder of the National Trust, Octavia Hill, was a key figure in the development of the COS, which is now known as the Family Welfare Association.
[39] Philpot, "Faithfull in her Fashion", p. 17.
[40] London Metropolitan Archives, EO/WEL/1/33.
[41] Abrams, *Woman in a Man's World*, p. 27.
[42] London Metropolitan Archives, Minute, LCC/EO/WEL/3/12.
[43] London Metropolitan Archives, Report, EO/WEL/1/25.
[44] Information from Karen Lyons, who started her working life as a

'School Care Organiser' in 1966.

[45] Abrams, tape transcription.
[46] The song, "Mother of hundreds and nobody's wife" was applied to Lucy Baroness Seear in the "Lord's Diary" when referring to Lucy in *The House Magazine*, Vol. 20, 667, (6 March 1995). It was originally a ballad by A.P. Herbert, called "Other People's Babies, A Song of Kensington Gardens", and goes:

> *Other people's babies*
> *That's my life!*
> *Mother to dozens*
> *And nobody's wife.*

[47] Letter, Dr Hugh Richards to LF 11 April 1979.
[48] Letter, Dr Hugh Richards to LF, to "Hon. MA", perhaps a reference to LF's Honorary Degree, and signed, "Much Love, Hon. Pa".
[49] Letter, 'B.' to LF, 11 December 1994.
[50] Denis Lawton and Peter Gordon, *HMI*, (London: Routledge & Kegan Paul, 1987).
[51] This is a summary of views expressed by Olive Stevenson in an interview with Niamh Dillon recorded for the National Sound Archive in 2004.
[52] Richard Titmuss, *Problems of Social Policy, History of the Second World War*, (London: HMSO and Longmans Green, 1950), p. 105.
[53] Bob Holman, *The Evacuation*, (Oxford: Lion Publishing, 1995), p. 11.
[54] Abrams, *Woman in a Man's World*, p. 28.
[55] BBC film, "*Where Were You on the Day War Broke Out?*", 3 September 1969, British Film Institute archive.
[56] Holman, p. 19.
[57] Draft Circular, National Archive, HLG7/130.
[58] Titmuss, p. 106
[59] Richard Titmuss, *Problems of Social Policy*, summarised in Packman, Jean, *The Child's Generation*, (Blackwell, 1981).
[60] Senior Regional Officer's Report no. 27. National Archive, HLG7/76.
[61] Geoffrey Shakespeare MP. Report of Commission on the Problems of Evacuation. (London: HMSO, 1941), para. 5-6. National Archive, HLG7/85.
[62] Manchester had been particularly successful in evacuating a high proportion of its vulnerable population.
[63] I think LF must mean the Dowager Duchess of Devonshire, of Chatsworth House, who was Evelyn Fitzmaurice, described by Pat Laurie, who was evacuated to Chatsworth with her school, Penhros College, as "ferocious and formidable".
[64] Holman, p.75.

65   Holman, p. 78.

66   Quoted in Titmuss, p. 163.

67   Circular 2596, 10 March 1942, quoted in Titmuss.

68   Shakespeare. para. 23.

69   Geraldine Aves, "Preliminary report on the development of welfare work", 5 May 1941. National Archive, HLG7/260.

70   Titmuss, Chap. 16.

71   Quoted in Titmuss, pp.168-9.

72   Holman, p. 127

73   Joel Kanter, ed. *Face to Face with Children. The Life and Work of Clare Winnicott.* (London: Karnac, 2004).

74   LF Archive, journal written December 1945.

75   Ibid.

76   Holman, pp. 51–52.

77   Ibid, p. 52.

78   Letter, Henry Maddock to LF, 9 January 1976.

79   Abrams, tape transcription.

80   As late as 1994 Lucy tried to find the report of this research and wrote unsuccessfully to the Greater London Record Office. She told Holman that Prof. Stone in Edinburgh had a copy, but I found no evidence that she had located it.

81   Holman, p. 87

82   Abrams, *Woman in a Man's World*, p. 30.

CHAPTER THREE

CIVIL SERVANT

Long ago in 1945 all the nice people in England were poor, allowing for exceptions. The streets of the cities were lined with buildings in bad repair or in no repair at all, bomb-sites piled with stony rubble, houses like giant teeth in which decay had been drilled out, leaving only the cavity. Some bomb-ripped buildings looked like the ruins of ancient castles until, at closer view, the wallpapers of various quite normal rooms would be visible, room above room, exposed, as on a stage, with one wall missing; sometimes a lavatory chain would dangle over nothing from a fourth- or fifth-floor ceiling; most of all the staircases survived, like a new art-form, leading up and up to an unspecified destination that made unusual demands on the mind's eye. All the nice people were poor; at least, that was a general axiom, the best of the rich being poor in spirit.

This is how Muriel Spark described post-War London in her novel *The Girls of Slender Means*.[83] Although fictional, the imagery conveys the visual landscape that confronted Lucy when she returned from Plymouth to London in 1945. By the end of the War, one third of the housing stock in England had been lost by enemy action.

Lucy and her mother and brother had been separated from each other for the length of the War. In 1940, with her daughter Lucy up in the Midlands doing good works and her son Leigh away serving in the army in the Far East, Bessie had decided to let the house in Howard Walk. She went to live with three women friends in a "very nice house" in Dorset.[84] Leigh had served in the Seaforth Highlanders.[85] A photo shows him in his kilt wearing owlish spectacles.

Lucy's brother, Leigh

Back in 1929–30 he had been in the Officer Training Corps at his boarding school, Canford, in Dorset. He had meanwhile been working as a solicitor's clerk, and was called up in May 1940, pronounced A1 fit, and sent for Infantry officers' training with the 11th Battalion, Gordon Highlanders. He was posted to India and Burma. From November 1943 to November 1944 he had been a Captain in the 14th Army 'Advanced Echelon'. Neither Lucy's papers, nor Leigh's army records give any details of his experiences, but the Seaforths were engaged in patrols through impenetrable jungle, mountainous terrain, monsoon mud and swollen rivers in search of the Japanese enemy. Even if Leigh had not been in the front line, disease, poor rations, lack of respite and extremes of climate were dangerous enemies. From November 1944 to May 1945, temporarily promoted to Major, Leigh had served at the HQ of the Allied land forces, South East Asia. The 14th Army, of which the Seaforths were a part, were famously known as the Forgotten Army as, for months after VE Day brought the fighting to a close in Europe, these men and women were still battling on in the Far East. The British gradually gained the upper hand, but Leigh and the Seaforths had left Burma before the dropping of the atom bomb on Hiroshima finally brought the war in Asia to a close.

In 1946, the little Faithfull family, mother, daughter and son, were reunited, returning to their house in Howard Walk, Hampstead Garden Suburb. This meant an easy commute on the Northern Line for Lucy as she resumed her LCC job in Islington. She comments:

> The fact that we were separated so much in our childhood strangely enough drew us together when we were adults. I know it has the reverse effect in some cases, but it didn't in our case.

Lucy had a conviction, born out of her personal experience and professional learning to this point in her life, that to separate children from their parents unnecessarily caused harm and pain. It is hard now to imagine that, in the mid-1940s, this was a new way of looking at things.[86] The Poor Law institutions and Victorian children's charities had been concerned to rescue children from harmful and corrupting influences in their homes, and give them what was seen as a brighter future. The evacuation of children during the War, although with the different aim of protecting children from physical injury from bombing and possible homelessness, had the effect of sometimes drastically severing the links between child and parent.

Meanwhile, amongst the swathe of radical social legislation that was enacted in the immediate post-War period, the National Insurance Act and the National Health Act for example, a key piece of children's legislation was in progress that was to have a major influence on Lucy's career. In a famous letter to *The Times* in July 1944, Lady Allen of Hurtwood had strongly criticised existing methods of child care. She pointed to the "chilly stigma of charity" and the "repressive conditions that are generations out of date" endured by deprived children, and called for an urgent public enquiry. Then, as the War was drawing to a close, the English public was scandalised to hear of the death of the young Dennis O'Neill at the hands of his foster father at Bank Farm, Minsterley. In 1945, Sir Walter Monckton reported on the circumstances of the 'boarding out' of Denis and his brother Terence, and highlighted a chaotic overlapping of administrative responsibilities for fostered children, and deprived children generally. Education Committees, Public Assistance committees, different local authorities, different central government departments, the Home Office and the Ministry of Health all had a finger in the pie. A Committee was set up under the chairmanship of Miss (later Dame) Myra Curtis, the terms of reference of which were to inquire into existing methods of providing for children "deprived of a normal home life" and to consider "what further measures should be taken to compensate them for lack of parental care". The resulting Curtis Report[87] formed the basis for the 1948 Children Act, a very important piece of legislation, which unified services for children into new local authority Children's Departments financed jointly by the Home Office and local rates, and headed by a Children's Officer. Centrally, responsibility for the welfare of children was passed from the Ministry of Health onto the Home Office Children's Branch.

Lucy had found her experiences as Regional Welfare Officer to be a burden of responsibility that weighed on her considerably. She told Abrams that, frankly, she needed "breathing space" from all that direct responsibility for children. The Children Act had set up a system for inspection of provision for children, and, after two further years with the LCC in Islington, in 1948, Lucy applied for and got a post as inspector in the children's branch of the Home Office.

In order to be taken into the new inspectorate Lucy must have made a very good impression while she was working with the evacuees. She may have been influenced to apply to the Home Office through her friendship with Clare Britton. Clare had many things in common with Lucy. She had also been a children's club organiser in the 1930s (and like Lucy, had been much concerned with provision of boots and shoes), and she had also worked with evacuees during the War, in a different area from Lucy, but they may well have met at meetings at the Ministry of Health. Clare was by now a Home Office inspector. She later married Donald Winnicott, the eminent child psychiatrist, and ran the child care course at the London School of Economics. She became an influential friend of Lucy's.

The people the Home Office wanted for this new inspectorial role, as described in the press advertisement,[88] would be between the ages of twenty-eight and forty, would hold "a University degree or diploma or certificate in social science or domestic science or institutional management [...] account will be taken of experience connected with the care of children, including the work of residential nurseries". The salary for a Grade II inspector, which Lucy was, was £575 + £30. Male inspectors earned £125 more, a sign of the mores of the time, but a large number of the appointments made were in fact women.

> "Being an inspector, one wouldn't carry the ultimate responsibility, and one would have more time to read and go to lectures, and at the same time earn a living and be in touch with the children, albeit at second hand", Lucy told Abrams. She went on to describe the job:

> As a Home Office Inspector one was given an area, and in that area you had to inspect local authorities' children's departments; you had to inspect the way the department ran administratively; you had to inspect their foster parent system, and visit foster parents; you had to visit children's homes, nurseries, approved schools, and submit reports following your visits. And in that way, to establish and maintain a standard of child care. [...] You would pick up good ideas from one place and then you'd visit another place and suggest to them that they might try what you'd seen elsewhere. So that you disseminated good ideas that you had learnt from various different people.

Eileen Younghusband, in her history of social work[89] writes that the Home Office inspector:

played a crucial part in discovering the needs of children in care, in supporting children's department staffs, helping to raise standards […] and themselves profiting from the experience of the best services […] they provided a consultant, reinforcing service across the whole field of child care.

Their own professional development was not neglected. Many took part themselves in in-service training and the training inspectors also participated in regular meetings with universities providing child care courses.

In this role, Lucy was very involved in the post-War process of reform that aimed to close the large Poor Law institutions where children lived a highly disciplined, institutional life, sleeping in large dormitories, with little one-to-one care, and replace them with smaller group homes with a house-mother and perhaps a house-father. "I can remember visiting [an institution] with twenty children in a dormitory, and with the place horribly clean, and very bright, so that you slipped on the floor", she said, before commenting on the emotional coldness experienced by the children. They received little individual care or attention. Lucy described to Abrams her weekly routine as an inspector:

You would get into your car, having planned your week, and you would visit perhaps a nursery in the morning and a home in the afternoon. Then you would perhaps visit a local authority, and look at the way they organised their work, and ask if you could visit foster homes with the staff. You would perhaps visit child-minders as well […] I used to be away for a whole week. Then the next week you would write up all your reports, and your reports would then go to the senior Inspector, and to the Administrator, and then arising out of your reports they would then write to the local authority and say, 'Our inspector says that […]' such and such a home needs to be looked at and should be reorganised, or they would write and say that the foster homes were not being visited regularly as they should be by law [...] So one did learn an awful lot.

Some of this learning must have been very valuable for Lucy in her subsequent career in local government as she must have gained valuable first-hand experience in dealing with government ministers and civil servants.

The immediate post-War period must have been an exciting time to be working in public services. William Beveridge was striding about proposing to slay his five giants of Want (by which he meant poverty), Disease, Ignorance, Squalor and Idleness. Beveridge had left his privileged background to become a social worker in the East End of London before the First World War. His Report, a runaway best seller, transformed the health and welfare structures of the country after the War, setting up the National Insurance system, which swept away centuries-old oppressive, patchy and unfair welfare provision. Meanwhile, Nye Bevan was undertaking the huge task of creating the National Health Service. The changes within the child care system were a less well known, but important part of the reforms of the age.

The Home Office handed out copious guidance to its inspectors. T. Paterson Owens, the Chief Inspector, issued a memorandum in 1948 that expresses the considerable early idealism with which the service was imbued. He reflects, I think, the post-War spirit that almost anything was possible in this new world. He writes:

> Each inspector will wish to develop those methods of inspecting and advising which best suit his [sic] own personality and the varying characteristics of those with whom his duties bring him into contact. It is natural and desirable that his initiative and interest, stimulated by personal observations and by his assessment of the various agencies of the children's services in action, will induce an eagerness to make an individual and personal contribution to the advancement of child welfare. Indeed, the welfare of the individual child must be the key stone

of our work, pursued through a combination of diverse media, as variegated and adaptable as the men and women who constitute the Service, from the individual foster home to the central organisation. [...] All will, I am sure, agree in looking for and striving for the achievement of such relationships between the children and persons or agencies responsible for them as will win for the children the greatest possible measure of present happiness and a growing preparedness to take their normal place in the life of the community.[90]

Given that the inspectors were to scrutinise a service for which they themselves had never had responsibility (because, of course, the Children's Departments and the Inspectorate were being set up simultaneously), the Chief Inspector clearly felt that the new inspectors needed comprehensive guidance as to how their reports of their visits to children's homes were to be framed. They should be "objective and should build up a background of factual information sufficient to aid the formation of a balanced judgement". He allows that "the question of standards of accommodation is complicated at the present time by the difficulties of building and shortages of material", and then goes into enormous detail about the headings for the reports. First should come the date of, and reason for, the visit, the number of children in residence and the number of places. Then should follow a series of numbered paragraphs detailing various aspects of the home: dormitories, washing facilities, food storage, staffing, religious instruction, rewards and privileges, record-keeping, 'homeliness', sex instruction, to name but a few. The concluding section was to be divided into headings: a) matters for follow up at the next meeting, b) recommendations to the Supervising Inspector, and c) matters apparently involving questions of policy for consideration by the Chief Inspector or otherwise calling for a decision or guidance." So Lucy's relieved statement that "if anything was wrong you handed it on to your seniors" was certainly the Home Office's expectation of her.

The regions were London North and South, Cardiff, Birmingham, Leeds and Manchester. To back up the voluminous written guidance, either the Chief Inspector or his Deputy aimed to visit each region once a month. Monthly meetings were also held between the Chief Inspector and his Deputies who, in 1948, were Miss Scorrer and Mr Revell, and the Superintending Inspectors who reported to them and were responsible for a geographical region. The actual inspectors, such as Lucy, reported to these Superintending Inspectors, but did not attend the meetings.

It seems that, certainly in the early days of her appointment, Lucy was assigned to the Central Training Council for Child Care within the Home Office because she was summoned to one of these monthly meetings on July 15th 1948. "Miss Faithfull of the Central Training Council Inspectorate attended." Miss Thackeray, Children's Officer for Devon, had complained that some trainees had been sent to one of the Homes in Devon without her knowledge. The minute reports:

> Miss Faithfull was invited to attend the discussion on
> this point; she explained the arrangement for enabling
> prospective boarding-out officers and housemothers
> who were being trained under a scheme approved by the
> Central Training Council to gain experience in Children's
> homes and similar institutions and said that when it was
> desired to send a trainee to an institution run by a local
> authority, an official letter was addressed to the authority
> asking for their agreement. The Devon Authority had
> been asked if they could accept three trainees (one man
> and two women) at the Newton Abbot Homes but had
> not felt able to meet the request.[91]

She added emphatically, "No students had been sent to any of the Children's Homes in Devon by the Home Office, without the prior agreement of the Local Authority". Miss Thackeray was put firmly in her place. I have spent a large part of my social work career trying to arrange practice placements for social work students in the face of frequent reluctance on the part of managers to add to their teams' workload, and it is depressing to read that

Lucy was having similar difficulties all those years ago.

Statutory inspection was only one part of the job. The other, equally important in "this immense new field in which our endeavour lies", was for each individual inspector to be an "advisor and helper of those responsible for the care of the children". In order to be this:

> he [*sic*] will wish to make his first care the establishment of a basis of mutual confidence, which will enable him to pursue his more detailed inquiries in an atmosphere free from restraint or suspicion.

Officials were moved around in true civil service style. Initially, Lucy was detailed to cover Berkshire where the Children's Officer was a woman about whose competency the Home Office had severe doubts. "Miss Summerhayes is not shaping up well and it looks as if the Berkshire job may be beyond her powers", says a memo by the Superintending Inspector, Miss M. Glyn Jones.[92] On April 27th 1954, Lucy visited Beenham Lodge where she found problems with the fire precautions. The next day, she was at Lilac Cottage and remarked that the water was heated on a very old-fashioned range. "Miss Faithfull [...] had wondered whether a modern one might not be more economical and make less domestic work". Miss Summerhayes was having none of it. The range was "perfectly efficient", and, furthermore, it was "a good thing for children to have equipment approximating to that found in their own homes, and she would include old-fashioned ranges in that category", reports Miss Glyn Jones in some despair. Were the children themselves stoking the range, one wonders? The authorities were nevertheless anxious to give the inadequate Miss Summerhayes every help, "so that should she fail it will not be for lack of support and advice from the Home Office".[93]

At some point in the early 1950s, presumably because Leigh had set himself up independently, Lucy and her mother moved from Hampstead Garden Suburb to a flat in Chelsea. They each had their own bedroom and sitting room, and a housekeeper, Mrs Mary Walker, was engaged to work five mornings a week.[94]

One of Lucy's main concerns was to see that the local authority child care officers carried out their duties with regard to foster parents. Prior to the 1948 Act, the standard of inspection of foster parents and the level of support available to them had been haphazard and patchy, and it was one of the consequences of the O'Neill case that supervision of foster placements was given high priority by Children's Departments. Early child care workers were zealous in trying to empty the children's homes and to recruit foster parents. John Stroud, who trained as a social worker in that period, described this proselytising enthusiasm:

> Our impression at the University was that the country outside was dotted with castle-like institutions in which hundreds of children dressed in blue serge were drilled to the sound of whistles. We were going to tear down the mouldering bastions [...] I had a dream of myself letting up a blind so that sunshine flooded into a darkened room as I turned, with a frank and friendly smile, to the little upturned faces within.[95]

I doubt if Lucy shared this naïveté, but she surely preferred family care to institutional care for children wherever possible.

The fifties was an eventful decade on the national scene. Food rationing finally ended, the Festival of Britain entertained a War-weary public, the Korean War began, Hillary and Tenzing climbed Mount Everest, Queen Elizabeth II was crowned in Westminster Abbey, Sputnik 1 was launched, the first protesters against nuclear weapons marched to Aldermaston, the Suez crisis tested Anthony Eden, and Harold Macmillan became prime minister in the age of 'you've never had it so good'.

Against this background, Lucy was moved away from the Midlands to cover Cambridgeshire, continuing to inspect residential homes for children. With all this travelling around the country meeting people, relating to different Children's Departments and, no doubt, hearing inspector colleagues talking about their areas, Lucy must have gained a wide overview of a number of authorities,

Lucy Faithfull

large and small, and the variations in standards of care offered to children. She would have learned a lot about the job of Children's Officer, and probably understood the important role played by the local Children's Committees. "Some committees were relatively moribund. In some small authorities you were likely to land up with fairly appalling local government members".[96] With her insider's view from the Home Office, she was ideally placed to make a good decision about which authority to join.

So, ten years after the 1948 Children Act brought the children's departments into being, she plucked up courage to apply to Oxford City to be their Children's Officer. This was a small and therefore manageable city authority. She probably shrewdly recognised that it was one onto which she could put her own stamp. Furthermore, it had a highly civilised, intelligent and capable committee, many of its members being university dons.

In 1958, Lucy was already forty-eight, and now felt she was ready for the "100 per cent commitment" of becoming individually responsible for children and staff. She left the safe confines of the inspector's role, and, over the next few years, she came to know most of the children in Oxford's Care personally as their Children's Officer, and resumed her role as "mother to hundreds".

Civil servant

Notes:

[83] Muriel Spark, *The Girls of Slender Means*, (London: Macmillan, 1963).

[84] Her Dorset address was *West Wind*s, Clarence Road, Dorchester.

[85] The Seaforth Highlanders were raised in 1793 "for the Defence of His Glorious Majesty King George the Third". Their recruiting poster invited "All Lads of True Highland Blood willing to shew their Loyalty and Spirit may repair to Seaforth [...] where they will receive High Bounties and Soldier-like Entertainment."

[86] Sonia Jackson, "Obituary. Baroness Faithfull 1910–1996", *Brit. Journ. Social Work*. 26, (1996) 447 – 450.

[87] *Report of the Care of Children Committee*, Cmd. 6922, (HMSO: 1946).

[88] National Archive, MH102/1493.

[89] Younghusband, Eileen, *Social Work in Britain 1950–1975*, (London: George Allen & Unwin, 1978).

[90] National Archive, MH102/1573.

[91] National Archive MF102/1574.

[92] National Archive MH102/1642.

[93] Ibid.

[94] Reference by LF for Mrs Walker.

[95] John Stroud, *The Shorn Lamb*, (Longmans, 1960).

[96] Jenny Fells, tape transcription of interview, 3 August 2006.

CHAPTER FOUR

MOTHER TO HUNDREDS IN OXFORD

The Curtis Committee had set out what would now be called the "person spec" for a Children's Officer, which fitted Lucy to a T. She (and it was to be a woman) should be a social science graduate, experienced with children, and with good administrative ability. "She should be genial and friendly in manner and be able to set both children and adults at their ease".[97] The expectation was that she should know all the children "deprived of a normal home life" personally, and be, in effect, a one-woman social work service.

In many local authorities, the idea of a female Chief Officer was a radically new, and largely unwelcome, one. Women in this position had to use to the maximum their wisdom, tact and diplomacy when dealing with male Medical Officers of Health and Directors of Education, both of whom probably thought that the children's service should have been given to them. In one Northern county borough, for example, the woman appointed was a trained almoner with a classics degree and a social sciences diploma. To her acute discomfort, she was offered a desk in the typists' room in the health department but, protesting about this, she was permitted to join the health visitors.[98] Lucy fortunately did not have to endure this extreme sexism.

The first Children's Officer for Oxford had been Miss Simpson, who had retired leaving the post vacant for Lucy. Miss Simpson, like many of the early Children's Officers, had a reputation for being formidable. It was she who appointed the young student Stella de Gruchy to work in Hernes House, one of the Oxford City children's homes, looking after eleven young boys. Stella remembers Miss Simpson as a large and imposing lady. She arrived at Hernes House one evening at about 7.30 "when we were completely exhausted having got the last little bleeder into bed, and she stormed in though the kitchen announcing, 'Do you know that the cat is in the frying pan?' I was dying to say, 'better than in the fire!'."[99]

Joan Glyn-Jones, who had been appointed as a Child Care Officer by Miss Simpson in 1956, considers that a great deal of the good work Lucy was to do in Oxford was based on foundations laid down by her predecessor. Miss Simpson's Deputy was Priscilla Young, later to become an eminent social work educationalist and head of the Central Council for Education and Training in Social Work (CCETSW) between 1971 and 1986. She left Oxford Children's Department just before Lucy was appointed.

Surprisingly, the question of Lucy's salary was not discussed at the time of her appointment. Her starting salary was £1175 per annum, much less than she had been earning at the Home Office. Perhaps this was of little concern to her, as she never mentioned it herself as far as I can determine, and the cost of living in Oxford was, I suppose, lower than that in London.

Lucy initially stayed with her Oxford friend Anna Toulmin, before organising her housekeeper in Chelsea to pack up the flat she and her mother shared there. She moved Bessie (now aged eighty-two) with her to Oxford, and the two women set up home in a substantial 1920s house on the Woodstock Road (*see right*). The house had light, spacious rooms with windows looking west over a large garden and the playing fields of St Edward's School and the Oxford Canal. She continued her pattern of employing part-time housekeepers, one of whom was Evelyn Fowler who was certainly with her in 1964.

Her brother Leigh, if not then, certainly a few years later, was working as a solicitor in Albany Court, Petty France, London. He also had a cottage in the ancient and unspoilt village of East Meon, near Petersfield, Hampshire, and he and Lucy visited each other frequently at weekends. 'Old Bell Cottage' overlooks the River Meon. The village is tucked into the Hampshire downs, and is dominated by a fine Norman church, which Lucy and Leigh presumably attended on Sunday mornings.

Lucy's house in Woodstock Road

An experience in Lucy's very first week as Children's Officer brought home to her the different role she was now expected to play:

> Sitting in my office I had a phone call from Bristol Juvenile Court saying, 'There's an Oxford child up in court and the Magistrates would like to make a Fit Person Order,[100] will you accept the Fit Person Order?' Well being a civil servant I said, 'I will certainly consider it and let you know'. And there was a howl from the other end of the phone, and the Clerk to the Magistrates Court said, 'The Magistrate's sitting here waiting for an answer'. I wasn't used to giving an answer straight away like that, and I thought well I'll be wrong positively rather than negatively, so I said, 'Yes, we'll accept it.' But I realised that when you are actually doing the work, it is quite different from working in the civil service, you had to ultimately

decide yourself, then and there very often, what you had to do.[101]

In the post-War period, a veritable revolution in the thinking about the welfare of children had taken place. John Bowlby's seminal book, *Child Care and the Growth of Love*,[102] had been published in paperback in 1953, and his emphasis on the importance of the attachment between a baby and its mother in the very early years, which is now generally accepted, seemed radical at that time. The psychoanalyst Donald Winnicott compared data collected during and after the War from both the UK and North America and found a striking common pattern of distressed behaviours among young children aged between one and three when separated from their mother for any extended period: first Protest, then Despair and finally Detachment, a withdrawn and passive state.[103] Both writers argued that physical proximity to a mother figure for the first two years of life is essential for the child's emotional and intellectual development. Donald Winnicott and his second wife Clare Britton, Lucy's friend from the Home Office, had both worked in the early 1940s in a hostel for troubled evacuees in Oxfordshire. Winnicott was also famous for developing the concept of the 'good-enough mother', which is parenting that is not necessarily perfect, but sufficiently consistent and loving to meet the child's needs and ensure healthy development. Lucy often referred cases to Winnicott and he also became a valued friend of hers, but, in any case, his thinking and writing chimed very closely with her own views, derived from her own early experiences of separation from her parents, and provided a theoretical basis for her work in Oxford Children's Department and throughout her subsequent career. "We sat at their [Bowlby and Winnicott's] feet", she told Abrams.

Over time, there had been developments in the philosophy underlying the care of children outside their own families. The first phase, going back to Thomas Coram in the eighteenth century, had been the idea that children could be cared for en masse in large institutions or orphanages. The exigencies of the large numbers meant that the daily routine was regimented, and dictated by the needs of the institution rather than those of the individual child. Children had little space, either physical or emotional, to play, have fun, or learn. They were also largely cut off from their family of origin. In the Victorian workhouses, for example, children were kept in a completely separate part of the building from their parents, and rarely saw them. Then came Dr Barnardo with his dream of small cottage homes set around a green, a sort of children's village. By the time Lucy came to Oxford, these ideas had been replaced by the theory that children were best cared for in smaller groups that more closely replicated the family unit, in houses in ordinary streets, with a housemother (with perhaps her husband as housefather) in charge. Underlying all three models of residential care was the idea that children needed to be 'rescued' from bad and neglectful parents, from deprived and poverty-stricken backgrounds, and given a new start in the care of the local authority. The role of the Child Care Officer was to support these children in their alternative homes. Also, by 1958, children were beginning to be 'boarded out', that is, placed with foster parents, who were largely recruited and supported by Child Care Officers. The frequency with which the Officers had to visit children in their care was laid down by statute.

As Children's Officer, Lucy was responsible to the Children's Committee of the City Council, and felt herself to be particularly fortunate, because she had "absolutely outstanding councillors" on her committee – she clearly thought of it as her own group. It was dominated by the Tories, (which would suit Lucy), who were supportive of the work the social workers were trying to do with individual people, helping them to adapt to "the wicked world around them". Although Lucy's Deputy, Jenny Fells, describes herself as "pretty left wing", she nevertheless feels the Oxford committee was more humane than many a left wing Labour-dominated committee with their working class solidarity. Mrs (later Dame) Janet Young[104] was a member, becoming Chairman [*sic*] in 1962, and was also a close friend of Lucy's. The status of the Committee locally and the level of its involvement was crucial to the success of the department. Jenny Fells pays tribute to the way in which Lucy handled her committee. She would do preparatory work, she would have a quiet word in the ear of the right person before the meeting so that the committee were already in support of her proposal, whatever it was, and she never had to engage in battles with them.[105] Stella de Gruchy adds perceptively, "she must have had defeats, there must have been things she wanted to do and they wouldn't, but she'd have just saved her powder and tried again another day."

Don Brand, who was one of Lucy's Child Care Officers, speaks of the extraordinarily detailed involvement by the Committee in the day-to-day decisions of the staff. He remembers having to go to one of the monthly committee meetings to ask for 7/6d for a pair of ballet shoes for a foster child to have ballet lessons.[106] Lucy could apparently authorise the lessons but not the necessary shoes. One small example of the support the Committee gave Lucy comes in the minutes of the meeting of 5th July 1960. "Resolved that the action of the Children's Officer in refusing permission to older boys at Hernes House to purchase motor bicycles by hire purchase be confirmed."[107] Behind this dry minute is concealed what must have been a lively debate with the boys, a firm decision and a perhaps amusing discussion in committee. Was it the motorbikes or the idea of hire purchase that was particularly disapproved of?

Even though it was administratively cumbersome, this close involvement did keep committee members in touch with children in their care as individuals.

After she had been in post for a year, Lucy wrote a comprehensive report to her Committee. She lists her staff: her Deputy was Miss P. McKay; her two Senior Child Care Officers were Miss J. Pollard, who had a Diploma in Public and Social Administration from Oxford University, and Mr J.H. Williams, a graduate of Swansea University who also had an Applied Social Studies Diploma from LSE. There were two Child Care Officers (CCOs), both of whom held a Home Office Child Care

Certificate. They all held caseloads and worked with the juvenile court, and, in addition, each had individual special responsibilities. It was Miss Pollard who was responsible for the finding and vetting of foster homes, Mr Williams for work with adolescent boys and training of male Child Care students, the two CCOs for adoption work, and for liaison with the children's homes. Lucy pays tribute to the long hours they all work and makes a plea for upgrading their posts. Much of the work of a CCO had to be done in the evenings and weekends, she argued. Children must be visited after they have returned from school, fathers and foster fathers must be seen after they return from work, and, on Saturdays, Officers often attended school functions of children in residential schools for whom they acted 'in loco parentis'.[108]

The conditions in which staff had to work in their offices at 10 Worcester Street sound truly dreadful. In June 1959, Lucy tells her Committee:

> In the wet weather the rain seeps into the Children's Officers' room; it percolates into the clerks' office and unless care is taken it causes damage to the files. One of the interviewing rooms has on occasions to be mopped out when the rain streams in. One prospective foster parent remarked, 'You demand a high standard from us, but the passage in which we have to wait and the room in which you have to interview us make us wonder about your own standards'.

Which Children's Committee member could resist such detail? But of course, as is the nature of local government, resources for righting these wrongs had to be granted by the City Architect and Estates Committee. Lucy piles it on:

> As a new Children's Officer I am filled with admiration and some wonder at the way in which the staff, particularly the administrative staff, have worked for so long under such conditions, and have worked well and without complaint. After ten years of such appalling

accommodation, I would on their behalf make a plea for some good offices to replace those in which the Department have worked uncomfortably and for so long."

Everyone struggled on, and, unsurprisingly, by December 1959, Lucy had to report the discovery of serious dry rot. The rehousing of the department became imperative.

Lucy inherited responsibility for a range of children's homes. 25 Maltfield Road had been set up as a Family Group Home for boys and girls, but had evolved into a Home for children attending Slade Park School for educationally subnormal children. The house still exists, no longer a children's home, at the edge of a quiet council estate in North Headington on low ground below the John Radcliffe Hospital. It is an archetypal 1950s children's home, larger than its neighbours, but designed to pretend to be a normal house like any other.

Hernes House had places for twelve boys aged five to seventeen years who were likely to be in care for some time. Of these, four or five were working boys. Lucy told her committee that:

> The boys in this Home are particularly difficult.
> Among them is a working boy who was at a school for
> maladjusted children, another who was at a school for
> educationally sub-normal children, and of the school
> children three are attending the Child Guidance Clinic,

She hoped to replace the two assistant housemothers with a couple. The husband would go out to work but receive "board and lodging and £100 a year for his services in the evenings, at weekends and during the holidays". The place sounds in urgent need of an upgrade. Lucy reports to her committee, "the dark brown paint and dark hall wallpaper make a somewhat dreary impression; the equipment is dull and much of it is old and battered". She ordered new dining tables and chairs, a new rug for the boys' playroom, a new washing machine and spin dryer, and £30 was collected towards a television set. (Much more fundraising for this followed.) "The staff have been asked to acquire stronger light bulbs", she adds. The redecoration was approved but one room soon had to be redone as one boy had "damaged the new paint by using the walls as a dart-board." (Perhaps this was a protest at not being allowed a motorbike?) Oh, dear. Lucy's plan was to make this a mixed sex home, entailing building an extra bathroom and WC.

Windmill House had been operating since October 1957 when it accommodated "the residue" of two other homes, with a children's nursery wing attached. There were places for thirty children across a wide age range. The idea was that children who were received into care and were not suitable for direct placement in a foster home should be admitted to be

> assessed as to emotional stability, intelligence, potentialities and needs. This involves not only a knowledge of the child as an individual but also in relation to the family. To this end a parent is encouraged to have contact with the child by frequent visits to the Home and outings with the child. Plans based on these assessments are made for the long-term care of the child. To this end Case Conferences are held once a month when the staff of the Home and the Child Care staff meet at Windmill House under the chairmanship of the Children's Officer for discussion on the child's behaviour, his family and his future.[109]

Lucy felt the building itself was fine. "The imaginative planning of the house in an L shape reduces to a minimum the impression of an institution".

> The wide age range allows children of one family to be together under one roof. Moreover there is also continuity of care. Thus at the age of 3–5 years, a child moves from the Nursery wing to a group within the same building and with the same staff at hand, instead of from a residential nursery to a Children's Home in another part of the city.

However, Lucy was concerned about the facilities for the staff.

The staff bedroom and sitting room were in the centre of the house, so "they have little privacy and are unable, even on their off duty days, to get away from the noise and demands of the children". She sets out her philosophy of staff care:

> It is the right and indeed the need of every individual that circumstances should allow them to develop their own personalities against a background of work and of personal interests and relationships. If residential work with children is to attract and keep people who are wide in their outlook and who have and can keep a balanced point of view, then staff must have a measure of privacy and peace.

An extension was planned, but this encountered some opposition from the Home Office inspectorate of which Lucy had so recently been a member. The inspector argued that as so many young babies were boarded out, there was no need for a nursery wing so this could accommodate the staff, and that the home should offer twenty rather than thirty places. There would then be no need for an extension. Lucy marshalled her arguments. Oxford had, she said, one of the highest illegitimacy rates in the country; Oxford had only two other homes, whereas other authorities had more; there were likely to be more children needing preparation for adoption, and if places at Windmill House were cut, an additional home might soon be needed. The Committee supported her and a compromise was reached.

One of her first acts as Children's Officer was to consult her opposite number in Reading with the idea of setting up a reciprocal arrangement for the provision of hostel accommodation for working boys and girls. Reading already had a hostel for girls, to which girls from Oxford could be admitted, and the proposal was for Oxford to set up a working boys' hostel, which would also admit Reading boys. By November 1959, Reading seems to have withdrawn from this arrangement and the Council were looking to negotiate something very similar with Oxfordshire County Council. A property was identified at 258 Iffley Road. The plan

Lucy Faithfull: mother to hundreds

was, when the hostel was ready, both Hernes House and Maltfield Road should become mixed homes for girls and boys. Children who had been too long at Windmill House could transfer, and Windmill House could revert to its intended purpose, a reception, therapeutic and assessment centre.

Keith Bilton tells a story which shows Lucy's detailed, hands-on approach. He was a CCO in Somerset and needed a placement in a Working Boys' hostel for a teenage boy named Jimmy. He phoned Oxford, and spoke to Lucy. She said, "Yes, we will offer this boy a place, and our Mr Bromley[110] who visits the hostel once a week will endeavour to see him if he's there, and we would want you to visit him less frequently, say once a month," a proposal to which Bilton enthusiastically agreed. Unfortunately Jimmy was not so amenable; he disappeared. Bilton was expecting the response he would have got from practically any other department, a call from the man running the hostel saying, "Your wretched lad has absconded, and good riddance, we're not having him back." Instead he had another call from Lucy herself, saying regretfully, "I'm terribly sorry, we have been so careless as to allow Jimmy to run away."[111] Such was her concern both for individual young people, and for maintaining good relationships with other departments.

The Department (and other neighbouring authorities) also had access to "Thornbury", an Oxfordshire County Council Remand Home in Kidlington. It was a young man at this home whom Lucy, as a campaigning member of the House of Lords, came to interview many years later while she was making a TV film about juvenile justice.

A recurring theme of Lucy's reports to committee was her efforts to improve the salary scales paid to residential workers, as well as their working conditions. Then, as now, it was very difficult to train and retain qualified residential staff, (who were, and are, paid very little and have little recognition by society for their important work), and there was a high turnover of 'housemothers'. She knew that if she couldn't pay decent rates, she would not be able to attract good quality staff.

Lucy kept a close personal eye on the homes in her area, as did many Children's Officers. If there was a period where a home was understaffed, she would lie awake at night worrying that the children were not getting the physical or emotional care they so badly needed. On one occasion, she was concerned that she had uncovered some highly undesirable behaviour by a residential carer at one of the homes:

> I had a feeling that something wasn't right there, and I used to drop into this children's home at very odd hours. And one day I dropped in [...] and couldn't find any staff, and I said to the children 'Where is Auntie, and Uncle?' And they said, 'Well, Auntie's out, and Uncle is bathing the girls upstairs'. And so I went upstairs, and I found an adolescent girl in the bath, with the man in the bathroom. Now, I'm not saying that he was doing anything, but [...] whether he was or whether he wasn't, this was a most unwise thing to do. And when I saw them the next day about this, I [...] simply said to them, 'I have to report this to the Committee'. And as a result of that, they resigned at once, and left within a month. So that I suspect that something had been going on there.[112]

This was in an era when sexual abuse of children in care was hardly ever acknowledged or spoken about. The 1980s and 1990s were marked by a series of revelations about sexual abuse by residential social workers on the vulnerable children in their care[113], but Lucy in the 1960s was ahead of her time in recognising the signs of sexual abuse and acting promptly to protect children. She would go on, in her old age, to pioneer treatment on a large scale for sexual offenders.

During Lucy's tenure at Oxford, there was an increasing emphasis on fostering for children in care, rather than residential care. The clear preference of the 1948 Children Act was to have children fostered (or 'boarded out', as the phrase was at that time), and Children's Departments' prestige on the national stage tended to be measured by the proportion of children who were boarded out rather than placed in institutions. Periodic reports published by the Home Office Children's Department plotted the national decline in the number of children living in homes. In 1949, 35% of children in care nationally were boarded out; by 1960, this had risen to 48% of a larger number.[114] However, in Oxford, as in most Children's Departments across the country, the proportion of children in care who were fostered was much lower than would be the case now. Lucy was a strong proponent of placing children, especially very young ones, in foster families rather than Homes. Many of her efforts with the Committee were aimed at improving the boarding-out rates paid to foster families.

By the time Don Brand joined the Department, Maltfield House had become a family unit for ten to twelve younger children with a single living-in housemother, and Iffley Road, which had been the working boys' hostel, now catered for older teenagers, preparing them for independence. He had a large number of older children on his caseload who were placed in Approved Schools.[115] These were residential institutions to which young people, mainly boys, could be sent by a court, usually for committing offences but sometimes because they were deemed to be beyond parental control. They were created by the 1933 Children and Young Persons Act out of the earlier 'industrial' or 'reformatory' schools. They were mostly run by voluntary bodies, under the overall supervision of the Home Office. As well as receiving academic teaching, boys were put into work groups for such activities as building and bricklaying, metalwork, carpentry and gardening, with the emphasis being on discipline, physical exercise, obedience and hard work. "It tended to be a fairly well-trodden path, they'd go through other parts of the children's system, and the juvenile court would eventually say, Approved School", Brand reports. He spent a great deal of time travelling round most of the Approved Schools scattered around the South of England, visiting the children in his care. This is not quite what Lucy told Abrams. "I think in the eighteen years that I was

in Oxford we only had about six children in all that time that
went to approved schools. The rest of them we looked after, in
Oxford, either in children's home or foster home," she maintained.
The facts bear out Brand's version rather than hers, however. In
September 1962, for example, Oxford City had nine children
placed in Approved Schools and three who were remanded and
awaiting a vacancy.[116]

As in all areas of the country, there were Oxford families that
failed to pay the rent and fuel bills, and eviction was threatened.
There was concern that children should not be separated from their
parents in these circumstances, and temporary accommodation was
usually provided. The homeless persons unit in Oxford was housed
in wartime barrack-like accommodation at Slade Park run by a
couple called Mr and Mrs Wilson. Mrs Wilson's claim to fame was
that she had been part of an all-woman jazz band during the War.
Brand recalls the situation in the huts:

> The whole family would be living in one room. I can
> remember talking to Lucy about the problems I thought
> that caused, including questions about how husbands and
> wives were expected to have a normal sex life, in the same
> room as their kids. It was something Lucy hadn't thought
> about. Once I raised this she could see that it probably
> would be a problem! So she worked towards getting Slade
> Park replaced by proper accommodation.[117]

By 1967, she had achieved this. A report she wrote in April
that year,[118] proudly speaks of a "Family Rehabilitation Centre"
at Garden House, 60 Hollow Way, Cowley, with self-contained
flats for four families and up to seventeen children, and rooms for
group activities and a playgroup. The aim of the centre was to help
these families to become "responsible tenants". Garden House has
now been demolished to make way for an access road to a small
development of box-like houses.

When Lucy first came to the department, she found that there
was only one male Child Care Officer, Mr Williams. This was not
unusual because there was a culture at the time that 'child care'

was women's work. Lucy determined to create a better gender balance in her staff because of the importance of providing role models for boys coming into care. Four or five additional CCOs had been employed, and the number rose to fifteen by the time the Children's Department came to an end. What is more, they were all professionally qualified, which was far from the case in other Children's Departments of the time.

In 1960, Olive Stevenson was appointed to begin the first professional training course for social workers at Barnett House, Oxford University. She remembers going to see Lucy to discuss the placement of students in the Children's Department for the practical aspect of their training. "I was thirty-one and full of beans but distinctly nervous about meeting Lucy", she recalls in her 'Lucy Faithfull Memorial Lecture' of 1997.[119]

> As I came into the room, [Lucy] sprang up from behind her desk, walking briskly towards me, extending her hand and saying in her inimitable way, 'My dear, how nice to meet you.' The warmth of her welcome is still with me thirty-five years later, as is her lightness of touch."

Lucy went on to provide Olive with excellent support all the time she was at Barnett House.

By 1962, her efforts to provide her staff with suitable, or at least dry, accommodation had at last born fruit. Offices were identified for the Department at 77–79 George Street, a rabbit warren of rooms above three or four shops, one of which was a shoe repairer's. One disadvantage of this setting was that people used to climb up the stairs to the Children's Department by mistake. "We used to come forward helpfully to see what their problem was, and they would give us their little tickets to collect their shoes!" laughs Jenny Fells. Its city centre location meant that it was convenient for clients to come in for interviews, and the CCOs saw clients in the office as much or more often than visiting them in their homes. Jenny admired the practice of one of the CCOs, Rosemary Wood, who always had two things written down after an interview: one for the client, which listed all the things that she and they had agreed they would do, and then a list of things for herself and what she had agreed to do. She gave a copy of this to the client so that they knew exactly what was going to happen.[120]

Adoption was also a big part of the Department's work. In the 1950s, adoption and fostering were seen as fulfilling quite different functions. Adoption was for white babies with no significant health problems whose parents requested it.[121] It was rarely considered for children in Care. The 1958 Adoption Act empowered local authorities to become adoption agencies. This made it easier to place children who were in Care, as well as those who were not, in adoptive homes. In the early 1960s, most Children's Departments appointed adoption officers and a panel to approve placements. Prior to 1967, there was a 'moral welfare' worker in post in Oxford. After she retired, an adoption and unmarried mothers' section was set up with four CCOs. One was responsible for the adoptions, and the other three, one of whom was Joan Glyn-Jones, dealt with the girls who came to the Department for help with their babies.

Workers in the Children's Department I have spoken to are unanimous in thinking that Lucy, with all her gifts and charisma, could not have achieved as much had she not had clear-thinking deputies who were able to take care of the detailed day-to-day running of the Department. Pat McKay was one such, a very different character from Lucy, very precise, yet:

> she thought the world of Lucy although they were so different; they worked absolutely hand in glove. Some people found it difficult dealing with somebody as diffuse as Lucy. She could give you information about a family and every detail would be wrong, dates of birth and so on. She'd be right on the essentials. Pat McKay didn't get annoyed.[122]

Don Brand remembers the expanded configuration of the department at the time he knew it, in the late 1960s. Lucy's Deputy was Jenny Fells, (who replaced Pat McKay in 1968) and the Assistant Children's Officer was Roy Hobart, who led

Lucy Faithfull: mother to hundreds

particularly on delinquency and links with the courts. There were three general child care officer teams, each with a Senior social worker and three social workers, and a Family Casework team with three people who worked intensively with problem families on a long-term basis. Then there was the adoption section, and a small section of two or three workers specialising in juvenile delinquents and the courts, although workers in the general teams also had young offenders on their caseloads.

When Lucy appointed Jenny Fells she initially expected her to hold a small caseload. This was perhaps because she herself was so keen to keep in touch with individual families. Jenny, however, felt she could hardly do justice to the needs of the clients as well as acting as deputy. She challenged Lucy on this, and found that Lucy listened. "She got the point. You never had to do battle with her. She wasn't that kind of person. She might not agree. You might lose an argument but it would never be with a punch on the nose," Jenny says.

Lucy knew every Child Care Officer personally. They were a small group. At her weekly staff meeting, everyone fitted quite comfortably into her office. In her old-fashioned way, she courteously called them all by their surnames, even the women, but nevertheless had a relaxed and approachable style of management. She had a way of making everyone in the Department feel valued. Don Brand reports:

> She would meet you in the corridor and she would say, 'You mustn't tell anyone else, Mr Brand, but […]' and would confide something or other. You'd then find that she'd said the same thing to at least a dozen other people in the department so each of them would be taken into her confidence, separately; each was led to believe that this was something special between you and her. Everyone knew that's what she did, so it was part of Lucy's way of doing things.

She treated everyone, at whatever level in the department, as an equal. She called everyone "my dear" (or collectively, "my dears").

She would treat secretarial workers and cleaners in the same respectful and informal manner as she treated the professionals in the department. Brand remembers that she was particularly affected by the sudden death of one of the Department's administrators, Ken Stevens. She'd had some kind of argument with him a couple of days before he died, and that particularly bothered her. She was very "cut up" about it.

Lucy created a culture of acceptance and valuing of the individual. People could admit to a weakness or an area of ignorance without fear of unpleasant repercussions. There could be criticism, but it was set in the context of being accepted and approved of. Joan Warren, the Family Caseworker, comments, though, that it was not OK to criticise Lucy. One weekend, Lucy was called out to one of Joan's families, and she decided to eject the husband from Garden House.[123] Joan thought Lucy should have consulted her first, and said as much. Apparently, Lucy treated her frostily for a number of weeks. It is possible, of course, that Lucy realised that she was herself in the wrong, which is always a painful realisation, and so was particularly hurt by Joan's challenge.

Lucy was also fearless. She had an inner confidence that carried her wherever she wanted to go. She was ruthless in using the contacts she had presumably made during her years in the Home Office. She was used to operating in the government machine, but it was unusual for a Children's Officer to feel they were on a par with Secretaries of State, and what is more, that the Secretary of State should benefit from her own wisdom. Ann Thompson, another CCO, tells of an occasion when she had placed a Lithuanian child with Russian Orthodox foster parents on a voluntary basis because the mother had been admitted to psychiatric hospital. Eventually the mother was pronounced improved and the child was to go back to her immediately. Ann had some reservations about a too sudden move, and went to discuss the case with Lucy. "My dear, you must go and see Mr So-and-So at the Home Office", was the immediate response. "Who me?" the astonished Ann asked. It was not 'I'll be in touch with the Home Office'. It would not occur to Lucy not to knock on the relevant door to get what was wanted. It was perhaps because she maintained contact with the policy network links she had established in the Home Office that she was able to create such a forward-looking Department.

Another aspect of her style was that she had the courage of her convictions. She supported her staff in what might have been seen as risky situations, if it was ultimately for the good of a child. Jenny Fells has a conviction, perhaps derived from Lucy, that, in residential care, the best appointments are not necessarily the safest. "You have to have a flair for working with children. It's not about being safe and careful but being a bit mad and being able to get through to them", she says. Once Jenny appointed a housemother who nowadays would be regarded as a Human Resources nightmare. She had been living in a hostel and been an in-patient at the Warneford psychiatric hospital, but "she had been in analysis and had very good reports and I took her on. We had our ups and downs and she could get a bit manic at times, but she was super with the girls and they adored her". Lucy characteristically offered her wholehearted support in this perhaps risky venture. She would always step in and support her workers, especially if she could see that there were likely to be nasty public consequences of a decision.

It was during the time that Lucy was Children's Officer for Oxford City Council that society first began to take on board the previously unthinkable possibility that parents, and other adults, were capable of inflicting bodily injury on young children. In the 1960s, the work of Henry Kempe[124] and others was bringing this into the realms of public acceptance. Lucy was quick to understand the implications of this for social work. She even invited Kempe to one of the regular Tuesday staff meetings during a trip he made to England to publicise his ideas. She also began to liaise closely with Dr Kit Ounsted of the Park Children's Hospital in Oxford who was starting to recognise the phenomenon of 'non-accidental injury' on children brought to him. The anonymous citation for Lucy's Membership of the Royal College of Psychiatrists in 1993 speaks of this time in her career:

It is perhaps difficult to remember that physical abuse was rarely recognised before 1960 and multiple fractures in young children were attributed to Caffe's Syndrome [...] Sexual abuse was still in outer darkness, banished for nearly 100 years by the misconceptions of Freud. Kit Ounsted was at the Park Hospital when Lucy was Children's Officer. He recognised abuse for what it was and between them they taught the junior doctors and others involved in the care of these damaged children. Sometimes the atmosphere at the Park would become a little too dramatic, but those evening visits by Lucy to help us with a child whose problems stretched our intellects and tore our hearts, were healing as well as inspirational.

Lucy told a story to Daphne Statham to demonstrate her belief in the importance of intuition in child care. One night she woke with a start at midnight, convinced that something awful had happened to a particular child. She worried that she couldn't do anything at that time of night, but, at the crack of dawn, she rang the family's CCO, who apparently demurred. Lucy said, "the father's a milkman, he'll be on his rounds, follow him". The officer found the child in the milk float, seriously hurt. The mother had inflicted the injuries, and the milkman, thinking it was not safe to leave the child at home, had taken it with him. Lucy immediately arranged for the child to be seen by a paediatrician.

Medical staff at the hospital and social workers in Lucy's Children's Department jointly developed ways of working with local families where abuse was being identified. Kit Ounsted set up a residential unit where parents and 'abused' or 'maladjusted' children referred by social workers could go for residential treatment. Many of these children would probably now be diagnosed as autistic, but that was a condition that was also barely recognised at that time. Don Brand feels that Ounsted was in some ways ahead of Kempe in recognising child abuse for what it was. Joan Glyn-Jones was one of the social workers who worked with Ounsted.

He seized on the idea of battered babies and saw them everywhere. I was worried. He was a highly emotional man. I liked him and got on well with him but he wasn't everybody's cup of tea. I don't think he got on well with Pat McKay for instance because Pat was too cool and too detailed. He, like Lucy, saw things in the round, the larger picture, but I think Lucy worked hard to keep on good terms with him. He was a fantastic man in many respects but not easy to work with, I guess.

Despite some differences in approach, (Ounsted could be dismissive of parents in a way that Lucy never was), Lucy and Kit actually developed a close friendship, and he continued to send her letters and updates long after she left Oxford Council.

The Curtis Committee and the 1948 Children Act had been primarily concerned with the welfare of children in care, but, over the years, the idea gained credence that preventing children coming into care in the first place was better for them and their families (and incidentally much cheaper for the Department). The first Family Caseworker had been appointed in Oxfordshire in 1952 and another in Oxford City the following year. The Eighth Report on the work of the Children's Department set out the logic of this:

> There are many ways in which children's departments seek to avoid the separation of a child from his family: often the help of relatives or neighbours is sought or the parents are advised about the various welfare services such as national Assistance, home helps and day nurseries, which may enable them to keep their children with them. Long and intensive case-work may be necessary to enable a family to keep together and maintain a reasonable mode of living ... and in the long run ensure that the children do not repeat their parents' mistakes.[125]

Lucy embraced this movement toward prevention with enthusiasm. Stella de Gruchy talks of her foresight in persuading her committee of the necessity for allocating resources to keep families together at a time when this was still an unpopular cause. People had doubts about "helping these ghastly families, supporting children in these terrible homes with these awful parents. Lucy could made the unacceptable acceptable. She could cast the cloak of her own respectability over all sorts of dubious causes."[126] Lucy got agreement to employ family caseworkers to work full time with families in a separate team, which was led by Mr Williams.

> That was where Lucy was innovative, because she had taken notice of the Quaker thing in the East End, Family Services Unit, which worked closely with families in difficulty; they got really stuck in, gave real and solid help. Enlightened people like Lucy were looking at that model, says Stella de Gruchy.

Unlike the CCOs, the Family Casework team did not work with children in Care. The workers were equipped not only with casework skills but also with toys and books, pots and pans, distemper brush, cleaning equipment and substantial supplies of rubber sheeting. It was long-term work. Lucy used to comment about those families that you needed to look for progress over three or four generations. As she believed, "a fence at the top of a cliff is better than an ambulance at the bottom".

In 1963, the Children and Young Persons Act was passed which confirmed this emphasis on prevention. Its influential Section 1 gave local authorities the power to give "assistance in kind or, in exceptional circumstances, in cash" to prevent children coming into care or before the juvenile court. This led to dilemmas with which generations of social workers have battled; in what sort of circumstances can a payment to a family be justified as preventing a child from coming into care or committing a crime; and how can these payments be differentiated from those from the Social Security system?

Lucy also had a great reputation for doing extraordinary things with volunteers. Many of them were in fact qualified social workers who were married to Oxford dons. Keith Bilton says:

They did pretty much what they might have done if they were employed, but for no money. Of course, they couldn't carry the same accountability, but Lucy would have felt confident enough to carry the responsibility on their behalf.

It must have been extraordinarily helpful for the department.[127]

Lucy believed that deprived and chaotic families living in poverty were not the only ones needing social work support. She felt strongly that you needed to be able to help well-off, upper class and high profile people with their difficulties. Perhaps helped by her position in the University City of Oxford, she was often called upon to help students who had problems with, for example, drugs or depression. Around the walls of her office she had the coats of arms of twelve or fifteen Oxford colleges at which she had been helpful to one or other of the students. She got to know Harold Wilson, for example, because one of his sons had drug problems while a student at Oxford. Through the psychiatric problems of students, Lucy also worked closely with the Warneford Hospital, one of two psychiatric hospitals in Oxford at the time, where students who had breakdowns or made suicide attempts often went for in- or out-patient treatment.

She made frequent attempts to recruit foster parents from among the more prosperous families of Oxford, petitioning her committee for extra payments for them.

> Such families feel that should they accept a foster child, that child should have equal opportunities with their own children. If their own children have […] particular types of recreation, holidays etc. then they would wish for the foster child to have the same,

she points out.[128] Not a point that a socialist Children's Officer would have felt important, I think. James King, (who was sent by Leila Rendel, founder of the Caldecott Community, on a few months' placement to the department) has a story that relates to this. He was asked to vet a prospective foster home, and, after doing his visits, he carried out what would now be called a police check. If the police found something, the Children's Department, for reasons of confidentiality, were not supposed to enquire what it was. The inexperienced James was being rung regularly by the impatient husband; how was he to explain the rejection? Moreover the man was an Oxford City Councillor.

> Lucy and I decided we had to break the rule and verify the crime with the police. Lucy went to the police and charmed them. The answer came back that, as a boy of fourteen, the husband had been caught scrumping apples.

I guess that foster father was approved forthwith.

This concern for the welfare of middle-class families also led to Lucy developing close links with George Lyward and Finchden Manor.[129] Lyward was a pioneering and charismatic educationalist and Finchden a battered old Jacobean manor house near Tenterden in Kent. Most of the boys who came to Finchden had been excluded from school for one reason or another. For some, it was an alternative to borstal, or psychiatric hospital. Boys who were labelled 'violent', 'compulsive', 'dishonest' or even 'psychotic' in the outside world were free to regress to a boyhood world of comics, cards, football, fishing, hobbies and horseplay. "Why not let them have back their childhood?" Lyward once asked. "Let them do all those things. If they don't do them now, they'll do much worse things later." There were no locks on the doors, no formal routine and no curriculum. Much of the therapy came simply from the spontaneous friction of community life. The challenge the boys all (unconsciously) faced was a slow journey from the unboundaried world of infancy towards a greater awareness and acceptance of others. In short, growing up. Lyward was often asked to take boys from public schools who had run into difficulties of one sort or another. "He and Lucy were real kindred spirits", says Brand. Lucy was a great supporter of therapeutic communities such as Finchden, and, after her retirement, became Trustee of the Caldecott Community, also based in Kent. In the House of Lords she persistently advocated for their continued funding in the context of public spending cuts, and for recognition of their value in turning young lives around.

Years later, in the House of Lords, Lucy became, Brand felt, an unofficial social worker in residence to the many elderly and sometimes infirm peers. "I used to go and visit her in the Lords, and they would constantly be stopping her in the corridors and pouring out their troubles". A characteristic aside by Lucy during long debates in 1988 on the Children Bill was to congratulate Lord Mottistone on becoming a grandfather.

A feature of Children's Departments across the country was that they were small enough for the Children's Officer to know most of the children in care personally. Lucy certainly did, to an extent that would seem extraordinary today. Her birthday was at Christmas time. Instead of partying with friends and family, she spent every Christmas day going round the Children's Homes visiting 'her' children. Her archive is full of letters from adults who had been in the care of the City, keeping Lucy updated over the years with their marriages and babies, their work and their travels.[130] People I spoke to who visited Lucy in her home in Woodstock Road often reported that, while they were there, the phone or doorbell would ring, and it would be a person who had been one of 'her' children. Lucy would drop everything and be completely involved in the news they were bringing. She was indeed a "mother to hundreds" in Oxford.

In January 1962, Lucy's own mother died. Lucy and Leigh were with her, and it was Lucy who registered the death. The loss of such a dear parent left a gaping hole in Lucy's life. One condolence letter that arrived a few days later reassured her that she had made her mother's declining years as happy as anyone's could be. Another from "Phylla" (perhaps Phillida Sawbridge?)[131] comments that the flat must seem very empty. Abrams asked Lucy to what extent her thinking about children's rights had been influenced by her mother. Lucy replied that, as a result of her mother's experiences as matron in a boys' school, she had:

firm ideas how you dealt with children, which was that

you really cared deeply about them […] She didn't think
it was fair not to give children structure, and she never
thought it was fair just to let children have their own way
all the time. Children were devoted to her.

This sounds very much as if her mother's views informed her
own. Her mother was a life-long Conservative voter, but "she
never went to meetings or anything like that. She wasn't a political
person at all". "She was very religious, but she was very quiet about
it", she added, and in this respect she could have been talking
about herself.

Canon Brian Mountford, vicar of the University Church
of St Mary the Virgin,[132] where Lucy was a member of the
congregation for many years, says she came regularly to eight
o'clock communion, but she disappeared after the service and
"didn't mingle". Despite this, he knew her as a "grand lady, but
not haughty, and a great leveller, bringing people together". She,
in turn, obviously thought highly of him, as she once put his name
forward to the BBC as a prospective provider of *Prayer for the Day*.
She wrote "We have found his sermons of value, showing insight
and sensitivity."[133] The BBC's response was to ask her to do it, one
Saturday morning.[134] Mountford thinks it is through her St Mary's
connections that Lucy got to know the Bishop of Oxford, Richard
Harries.[135]

Very few people I talked to who worked with Lucy
professionally knew anything about her private life. She was
friendly with everybody, but would have thought it unprofessional
to make especial friends among her colleagues. She did become
good friends with Anne Wain (whom she appointed in 1960)
and her husband Tony. Anne had four children, and Lucy loved
watching them grow up. Lucy would visit the Wains at their house
in Headington, and they stayed friends until Anne's death in 1995.
Jenny Fells remembers going over to the local pub sometimes with
Lucy at lunchtime and meeting Lucy's great friends Beryl Hughes,
by now an Oxford magistrate, and her husband Bill, head of
Ruskin College. The Hugheses held their Golden Wedding party

in Jenny and Stella's house. Bill had been an MP so there were politicians among the guests. Jenny reports:

> It was a beastly wet day and we had expected to be out in the garden, but the whole house was taken over. I remember Barbara Castle eating her lunch on a bed. But the loveliest thing was Lucy. She said very determinedly, "I'm going outside", put her mac hat on and led a little party out – they were all sitting under a tree getting dripped on!

Back in late 1947, Oxford City had successfully resisted pressure from the Home Office to make a joint appointment of Children's Officer with neighbouring Oxfordshire. In 1951, the county had chosen the formidable Barbara Kahan as its energetic Children's Officer, a woman who was later to cross swords with Lucy.

Her philosophy and that of Lucy had notable similarities; the importance of employing qualified staff, the need for improvements in residential care for children and the importance of work with families to prevent children having to come into care. Kahan, like Lucy, had made pioneering use of the Park Hospital to identify and treat child abuse before it was generally recognised. However Kahan and Lucy could not be more different in personality and also in political persuasion. Where Lucy achieved her ends through charm, a close awareness of the feelings of other people, and political astuteness, Kahan could be ruthless and forceful in pursuit of her aims. The two women were in competition with each other to run the most effective Children's Department in the country. Unlike Lucy, Kahan would take her committee head on, although they were perhaps not such an amenable bunch as Lucy's committee. It could be that Kahan had 'a tougher row to hoe'. Kahan told Bob Holman that "The [Children's Committee] chairman was a railway signalman, and I was told by the clerk of the council that if I wanted with talk to him I could go to the signalbox". Kahan made a conscious decision to be a 'battleaxe' rather than a 'nice girl' who would be patted on the head and ignored. "What else could I do if I wanted to achieve anything?"[136] she asked rhetorically. Lucy used quite other tactics. She was the 'nice girl' personified, who used her charm, diplomacy and 'people skills' to get her way. "Lucy disguised her forcefulness".[137] So it was hardly surprising that Kahan and Lucy just did not get on. It is likely that the enmity originated with Kahan,[138] but, in the view of many who knew them both, it was a tragedy because, had they been able to work together on the many issues that concerned them both, they could perhaps have achieved even more than they each did individually.

There were other exceptionally creative and positive senior people in Oxford who worked closely with Lucy. The Medical Officer of Health was Dr Muir Grey. Jenny Fells describes his unexpected arrival with his bicycle clips on, wearing an eccentric 'scotch' hat, and instead of the usual tie, "a funny sort of scarf, and he reminded me of Lucy in some ways. He would go to anyone from the House of Lords to a down-and-out in the streets to get any information he needed to make his case". The Chief Probation Officer was Ken Thompson, who was "absolutely adorable", and apparently played the clown at the Christmas parties held every year and which included Kahan and her Oxfordshire county staff. There was a general atmosphere in Oxford of senior people across the board putting resources into constructive and creative ways to tackle difficult problems.

Both Oxfordshire and Oxford City Children's Departments built up a reputation for excellence in child care. Not all Children's Departments were as successful; there was a wide variation in their effectiveness. Some were just too small. The legacy of the Children's Departments for the subsequent development of the social work profession has been a subject for debate. Bob Holman points to the way in which the previous Public Assistance philosophy, which saw children as a ready source of domestic labour or as entrants to the army, was replaced by a more personalised and child-centred service, which saw children as individuals in their own homes. Holman also points out:

> The Children's Departments brought natural parents into

the state child care process. In the past, deprived children had often been 'rescued' from their parents, with both the Poor Law agencies and voluntary societies acting on the belief that, if the parents ceded the care of their children, then they were failures who should have no more influence over them.[139]

Leading child care thinkers, such as Clare Winnicott and Barbara Kahan as well as Lucy, understood that children did better when they could keep in touch with their natural families, and also that parents did not want to abandon their children but loved them and usually wanted them back.

Good Children's Departments attracted a group of highly motivated and professionally trained women to carry out this work, who saw their responsibility and their skill as knowing, caring for and communicating with children. This personal approach was unusual in the otherwise often overly bureaucratic local authorities. They also became skilled in negotiating with other agencies that had an impact on the lives of families, the Housing Departments, Education Departments, the courts and the police, for example.

However, there were also disadvantages in that Children's Departments were separate from the Welfare Departments whose clients were disabled or elderly people. Mental health was dealt with by yet another department. Many families' problems spanned these three, and there was no one door upon which they could knock. It did not make good sense to divide people into three such separate categories in their search for support. Also, the initially clearly defined role of Children's Departments had come under strain by successive moves towards more preventative work, efforts to return children in care to their own families, and the inclusion of young offenders (then known as juvenile delinquents) in the child care system. Jean Packman argues "it was this absorption of delinquents in to the mainstream of child care [which] finally brought the Children's Departments to an end."[140]

Legislation played its part in vastly increasing demand on local authority services, and hastening the end of the Children's

Departments. In the Welfare field, the Chronically Sick and Disabled Persons Act of 1970 gave local authorities responsibility for identifying all the 'handicapped' people in their areas and providing a range of services for them. The 1969 Children and Young Persons Act gave local authorities much wider responsibility for children in trouble, with its emphasis that juvenile offenders should be kept out of the criminal justice system as far as possible. It replaced 'Approved Schools' with Community Homes with Education, and introduced 'Intermediate Treatment', a raft of schemes designed to 'treat' rather than punish children in danger of coming to court. All these developments, however desirable in themselves, led to an increase in demand for the services of the department, with the consequent need for increased staffing. Children's Officers appointed deputies and assistants; senior social workers were brought in to supervise child care officers, and middle management arrived.

Over the previous decade, there had been various moves towards reform of local government structures. In 1959, the Younghusband Report recommended a common basic training for all social workers in Health and Welfare Departments. In the field of education, the Newsom and Plowden reports urged simplification of the local authority structure, and the Robbins report led to the expansion of higher education. The Maud Report on Management in Local Government of 1967 wanted a reduction in the number of small departments and committees into a mere five or six. Jean Packman in her history of the period says that Children's Officers nationally wanted any changes to be very gradual. The forum for their discussions was the Association of Children's Officers (ACO), formed in the wake of the 1948 Children Act. Packman says that they feared the loss of the very personal service, and the long-term parental type of involvement in which Children's Departments specialised.[141] There may well have been ambivalent feelings among them, and Lucy may well have shared these, but the line taken by their professional association was perfectly clear. It was in favour of reform.

In December 1965, a government committee under the chairmanship of Frederick Seebohm, later a friend and ally of Lucy's in the House of Lords, was appointed with a brief: "To review the organisation and responsibilities of the local authority personal social services in England and Wales and to consider what changes are desirable to secure an effective family service." Sylvia Watson, the then President of the ACO, met Seebohm at an evening function on the day his report was published. She found him "relieved and thankful that his mammoth task was completed". He recommended that each Local Authority should have a Social Services department, which would provide social work services to all client groups, and therefore bring children's services under one umbrella together with services for elderly people, for people with physical or learning disabilities and for those with mental health difficulties. It would mean the merging of Children's Departments with the Welfare and Health Departments.

One concern of Children's Officers was that the Welfare and Health departments were much dominated by a health rather than a social work perspective, and that the strength of the health lobby would push aside the emphasis on the social aspects of people's welfare that the Children's Departments had exemplified. There was a strong view that it was vital that the new Director of Social Services had a social work background (and also preferably management training). A chief opponent to the Seebohm ideas was the Association of Municipal Authorities which argued that each local authority should be able to make their own arrangements as to what department it would create and whom to appoint as chief officer. Some authorities, alarmingly, started to amalgamate health, welfare and children's departments under the Medical Officer of Health.

Throughout her time as Children's Officer, Lucy had become increasingly active in the Association of Children's Officers. This was effectively her peer group. From 1968, when she became Junior Vice-President, she was so busy on the Executive Council and its various sub-committees that a less energetic person would have had a hard time finding any time left over for running her own department.[142]

A Special Meeting of the Association of Children's Officers Executive Council on 1st February 1969 expressed concern about "anti-Seebohm developments" and appointed Lucy as a member of the Steering Committee of a "Seebohm Implementation Action Group" (SIAG) based in London and chaired by Tom White, Director of Social Services for Coventry. He explains the position of the ACO members at the time:

> They were more interested in a family focus on children than they were on a comprehensive service, but I think they quickly realised that they had to work for implementation as proposed or they would be stuck with the status quo. Lucy was one of the early ones to see that and I think also influenced her colleagues in that regard. [...] At first I was a bit suspicious to be frank, because there hadn't been total enthusiasm in support, but she soon dispelled that and was a very hard working and influential member [of SIAG].[143]

Tom White developed a sophisticated campaign. He obtained some funding from the National Institute for Social Work. SIAG members visited their MPs in their constituency surgeries to ensure they were properly briefed, and there was a mass lobby of Parliament by social workers. Notes were produced for public speakers. He valued Lucy's contacts with eminent people from Oxford and the Civil Service and they planned a strategy of who should approach whom. Such lobbying was uncommon in those days.

In her role in the SIAG Lucy wrote a stinging letter[144] to Mr Swaffield, the Secretary of the Association of Municipal Authorities. She argues that appointing a Director of Social Services who is not a social worker should be as unthinkable as appointing a Director of Education who is not a teacher, or a Medical Officer of Health who is not medically qualified. Typically for Lucy, she arranged to meet with him personally to discuss the issues and was to use her charm and persuasiveness against this seemingly intransigent opponent. Again, in late 1969, she wrote on behalf of the SIAG to James Callaghan and Richard Crossman, then Secretaries of State for respectively the Home Office and Social Services under Harold Wilson, urging the early implementation of the Seebohm report.[145] A draft letter was drawn up for individuals to send to their local MP along the same lines. The ACO issued a press release urging the Government for a statement of intent on Seebohm. Attempts were made to gain national publicity for the issues, but then, as now, social work was evidently not seen by editors as a subject likely to interest readers. Dorothy Watkins, Children's Officer for Cornwall writes:

> We are outraged by the unwillingness of [*The Times*] to publish letters either from Child Care Associations or even well known personalities concerned with social services […]. Lucy Faithfull, our present President, has made great efforts about this and […] just felt there was a complete lack of interest.[146]

Meanwhile, meetings were going ahead between Children's Officers and their opposite numbers in Welfare Departments. Lucy planned a study weekend for the ACO Council in Oxford, "in view of the many developments taking place."

In 1969, she became the very active (and penultimate) President of the ACO, so had a crucial leading role in the profession during this time of turmoil. Her Presidential Address to the ACO Annual Conference in Oxford that September was a *crie de coeur* for a distinctive social work contribution to the new world of social services.[147]

The Seebohm changes were, of course, not the only issue to occupy Lucy's energies and interests in the ACO arena. There were regular meetings between ACO representatives and the Chief Inspector and Supervising Inspectors at the Home Office. Lucy must have felt at home at these gatherings, given her previous Home Office inspection experience. She was moving in eminent company as Joan Cooper was Chief Inspector and Clare Winnicott an 'assessor'. At one of these meetings, on 14th December 1967, Lucy raised the issue of the importance of the police making full inquiries into the background of potential adopters.

Adoption was indeed one of her main areas of interest. She drafted a long report for the Home Office as evidence for their "Enquiry into Adoption Law and Practice" in late 1967. This proposed the setting up of one Tribunal to consider all adoption matters. This proposal was scrapped quite swiftly following representations from London North branch (of which, incidentally, Lucy was a member), but this is an early example of Lucy's interest in the idea of a single family court. The Home Office continued consulting professional bodies on adoption changes, and, in the autumn of 1968, Lucy attended a meeting for the ACO with the Home Office Joint Committee, among whose members were none other than Dame Eileen Younghusband.[148] Lucy also represented the ACO at several other meetings and "played a most active part in bringing the Association of British Adoption Agencies into existence" in 1970.

Another area of interest, which she carried over from her ACO days to her later Parliamentary career, was work with very young children. She argued for a Government enquiry into the needs of pre-school children. Baroness Bea Serota, then Minister of State at the Department of Health and Social Security, wrote a typically non-committal reply on the grounds that the government was not yet clear on its position on the Seebohm and Maud reports. One can imagine Lucy's impatience with this stalling, and, in fact, she never managed to get a comprehensive national review of care for pre-school children.

The ACO Annual Conferences were big events. At a conference in Harrogate in 1968, we see Lucy lording it on the high table at the Hotel Majestic with James Callaghan (then Home Secretary), Lord Kilbrandon,[149] social work luminaries such as Joan Cooper and Mia Kellmer-Pringle, and eminent Children's Officers such as Sylvia Watson.

The National Bureau for Co-operation in Child Care[150] set up a group to study the needs of 'handicapped children'. Needless to say, it was Lucy who co-ordinated ACO members' comments and wrote up their report to this group. She was critical of the Bureau group's initial questionnaire which, she felt, reflected an "unfortunate bias" by seeking information about the medical and educational needs of the handicapped child, but not the "social and emotional needs", the especial concern of the Children's Officers. Her report is far-sighted and anticipates many of the ideas later to be put forward in the Chronically Sick and Disabled Persons Act. She is strongly against disabled children being sent away to distant boarding schools; she advocates for better services for families where a young child is diagnosed with a disability, and for mildly handicapped children to be integrated into normal schools.[151]

"Children in Trouble" was the title of a White Paper that became the 1969 Children Bill. Lucy was appointed to an ACO sub-committee with the brief to "take appropriate action during the passage through Parliament of the Children Bill". This must have been invaluable experience for her to call upon twenty years later when she was deeply involved as a Peer of the Realm in "taking action" around the 1988 Children Bill.

Lucy's work in the area of Matrimonial Proceedings shows her ability to succinctly grasp highly complex matters, set them out clearly, and suggest constructive solutions to perceived problems. She wrote a report for the June 1969 Council on "Difficulties of Children's Departments in Respect of Matrimonial Proceedings in High, County and Magistrates courts." She gives vivid examples of the confusion and duplication caused by the overlap of responsibilities between Divorce Court Welfare Officers, (who were Probation Officers), and Children's Department social workers. In civil matrimonial matters, where children were already known to the Department, or even placed in foster care, there was often confusion about which officer should write court reports, and courts were often making judgements with no reference to the Child Care social worker involved. Worse, from the child's point of view, the court sometimes appointed a Probation Officer as supervisor, when the child was already supervised by a social worker, so for example, two different professionals could turn up at a foster home unbeknownst to each other – a very effective way of confusing a child and bemusing a foster parent. Lucy urged that a Home Office Memorandum of Guidance for Court Welfare Officers (which had previously only been available to the Probation service) be redrafted to sort out these matters, and, importantly, be made available to Children's Departments. The Home Office took its time "considering" this proposal, and it was not until the following summer that it got around to circulating the revised Guidance to Children's Officers.[152]

It must have been as part of her concern to ensure that her own Child Care Officers and residential staff had both professional training and adequate salaries and terms of employment that led her to concern herself with training and service conditions on the national stage. Among the very many meetings she attended in the Autumn/Winter of 1969 was one between the ACO, the Association of Child Care Officers (ACCO), and Home Office inspectors about the need to improve the quality of recruits for training into the profession. The minutes, reflecting her vivid use of language, report,:"Miss Faithfull said that in her opinion improvements in salary and sorting out the salary scales jungle was a basic necessity for the improvement of the service." At a May 1970 meeting with the Local Government Training Board at Alembic House, Albert Embankment, she pursued this issue of new training for social workers adapting to the Seebohm changes. The "new Council for Training in Social Work"[153] would arrange courses for social workers. Particular courses for newly appointed Directors and for middle management would be provided at LSE and the Birmingham Institute of Local Government Studies. Birmingham is where Lucy was soon to do her own management training. This concern with the quality and length of social work training was another interest that she carried forward to the Lords.

In all this work for the ACO we see Lucy passionately involved in nearly every issue facing the social work profession at the time. (She was also interested in improving the quality of residential child care, but as this was a particular speciality of Barbara Kahan's, she seems to have taken a back seat in discussions and policy on this issue.) The President's Diary for 1970 shows her doing something nearly every week of the year for the ACO. She can have had hardly any time when she was not working on one issue or another, and, at the same time, she was running her Department. Her whole life must have been devoted to work. Perhaps that was her way of dealing with the empty house following the death of her mother, or perhaps she just loved her job. I suspect the latter.

Notes:

[97] Report of the Care of Children Committee, Cmd. 6922, (HMSO, 1946), para. 446.

[98] B. Rogers, & J. Dixon, *Portrait of Social Work*, (Oxford University Press, 1960), quoted in Younghusband 1978, p. 38.

[99] Stella de Gruchy, tape transcription of interview, 3 August 2006.

[100] The Children and Young Persons Act 1933 gave the courts power to commit a child deemed to be in need of care or protection for whatever reason or children found guilty of an offence to a "fit person" as an alternative to approved school care. That 'person' was usually the local authority, embodied in the Children's Officer. The Act specified that "the person to whose care a child or young person is committed shall [...] have the same rights and powers and be subject to the same liabilities in respect of his maintenance as if he were his parent."

[101] Abrams, *Woman in a Man's World*, p. 31.

[102] John Bowlby, *Child Care and the Growth of Love*, (Harmondsworth: Pelican, 1953).

[103] Donald Winnicott, "The Nature of the Child's Tie to His Mother", *International Journal of Psycho-Analysis*, (1958).

[104] Lady Young was to become the only woman to serve in Mrs Thatcher's cabinet. In her later years she gained some notoriety as a champion of traditional Christian family values, opposing adoption by unmarried couples and the lowering of the age of consent for homosexual men.

[105] Jenny Fells and Stella de Gruchy, tape transcription of joint interview, 3 August 2006.

[106] Don Brand, tape transcription of interview, 9 November 2005.

[107] Minutes of the Children's Committee are held at the Oxfordshire County Archive, St Luke's Church, Cowley Road, Oxford.

[108] Oxford City Children's Department minutes, Oxfordshire County

Archive.

[109] Oxfordshire County Archive, Report to Children's Committee, 7 April 1959.

[110] John Bromley, later to become Director of Social Services in Doncaster.

[111] Keith Bilton, tape transcription of interview, 15 March 2006.

[112] Abrams, tape transcription.

[113] Some of the most notorious of these were the 1989 report into the Staffordshire "Pindown" scandal, the case of Frank Beck who was convicted in 1991 of abuse while he was officer-in-charge of children's homes in Leicestershire, and the 1996 Waterhouse inquiry into widespread abuse over a long period in children's homes in Clwyd and Gwynedd.

[114] Younghusband, 1978, p. 40.

[115] Approved Schools were abolished by the 1969 Children and Young Persons Act, and replaced by so-called 'Community Homes with Education' – CHEs.

[116] Oxfordshire County Archive, Children's Committee Report, 1962–64.

[117] Don Brand, tape transcription of interview, 9 November 2006.

[118] "Measures to prevent homelessness and to provide accommodation for homeless families", Modern Records Centre, University of Warwick, MSS.378/ACO/CO 4/7.4.

[119] Olive Stevenson, "50 Years of services to children in need of care: What have we learnt for tomorrow?" Lucy Faithfull Memorial Lecture, St Anne's College, Oxford. (Barkingside: Barnardo's, 1997).

[120] Jenny Fells, tape transcription of interview, 3 August 2006.

[121] June Thoburn, Trends in Foster Care and Adoption, in Stevenson, Olive (ed.) Child Welfare in the UK, (Blackwell Science, 1998), p. 121.

[122] Joan Glyn-Jones, tape transcription of joint interview, 21 April 2006.

[123] Garden House was the pioneering rehabilitation centre/hostel for homeless families.

[124] C. Henry Kempe et al., "The Battered Child Syndrome", *Journal of the American Medical Association*, 181, (1962), pp. 17–24.

[125] Eighth Report on the Work of the Children's Department, (Home Office, 1961), para.9. Quoted in Younghusband, 1978, p. 41.

[126] Stell de Grucy, tape transcription of interview, 3 August 2006.

[127] Keith Bilton, tape transcription of interview, 15 March 2006.

[128] Children's Committee Minutes, 5 November 1963.

[129] For more about Finchden Manor's pioneering work, see Michael Burn, *Mr Lyward's Answer*, London: Hamish Hamilton, 1956.

[130] A typical reply from LF to one of these letters, from 'Heather' reads, "thirty-five years ago seems a long time but those were happy days at

Windmill House. I still hear from Mr & Mrs Llewellyn and several of the children. Yours ever, Auntie Lucy." Letter, 6 September 1993.
Another letter is from a worker in the laundry at Littlemore Hospital to LF: "I must thank you for taking an interest in my welfare all the years you have known me, and I have great faith in you with all the kindnesses you have done for children in the children's homes like myself." 20 April 1981.

[131] Phillida Sawbridge had worked at Thomas Coram, before moving to the Post Adoption Centre. According to a very friendly letter from LF to her they had worked together in Brixton 'in that funny little office', and LF regrets not being able to attend her leaving party. Letter LF to PS, 26 May 1994.

[132] It was in this church that a sermon by John Keble in the 1830s started the (high Anglican) Oxford Movement.

[133] Letter, 18 August 1993.

[134] Letter, BBC to LF, 3 September 1993.

[135] Now Lord Harries of Pentregarth, a frequent contributor to the morning *Thought for the Day* slot on BBC Radio 4..

[136] Bob Holman, *Child Care Revisited: The Children's Departments 1948-1971* (London: Institute of Childcare and Social Education UK, 1998), pp.55-56.

[137] Keith Bilton, tape transcription of interview, 15 March 2006.

[138] In the opinion of Daphne Statham, ex-Director of the National Institute of Social Work (NISW).

[139] Bob Holman, *Champions for Children*, p. 167.

[140] Jean Packman, *The Child's Generation*. 2nd edit. (Oxford: Blackwell and Robertson, 1981).

[141] Jean Packman, Chap. 8.

[142] In 1967, for example, she had represented the ACO on the Association of Municipal Corporations, and at meetings on adoption with the National Council for Voluntary Child Care Organisations. In 1968, she served on the Training Committee of the ACO (convenor of which was Barbara Kahan), and was herself convenor of the Adoption Law Reform sub-committee, the Joint Committee on Adoption Practice, the working party on handicapped children, and of the sub-committee charged with arranging the 1969 ACO annual conference. (Modern Records Centre, University of Warwick, MSS.378.ACO/CO/1/12).

[143] Tom White, tape transcription of interview, 13 December 2006.

[144] Modern Records Centre, University of Warwick, MSS.378/ACO/CO/1/13.

[145] Letter from LF to David Fleet, Director of Social Services, Tower

Hamlets, 18 January 76.

[146] Letter from D. Watkins to E. V. Falk, 11 February 1969.

[147] "*Proceedings of Twentieth Annual Conference. Theme: A Family Social Work Service*". The Association of Children's Officers (Oxford, 17–19 September 1969).

[148] Eileen Younghusband (1902–1981) was internationally known for her research and teaching in the field of social work. The Younghusband Report of 1955 recommended generic social work training, a set of knowledge and skills common to all social workers. She was made a Dame in 1964. Her background was in many ways similar to LF's, and LF wrote the entry on EY in the *Dictionary of National Biography*.

[149] Lord Kilbrandon chaired a committee that recommended, in 1968, the setting up of the Scottish children's hearing system.

[150] Now known as the National Children's Bureau. Lucy had been present as representative of Oxford City's Children's Committee at the first Council meeting of the Bureau on 20 March 1964.

[151] Modern Records Centre, University of Warwick, MSS. 378/ACO/CO/1/12.

[152] Modern Records Centre, University of Warwick, MSS.378/ACO/CO/1/14.

[153] Set up as a result of the Younghusband Report and later known as the Central Council for Education and Training in Social Work (CCETSW).

CHAPTER FIVE

"THE LUCY SHOW"

In the event, the government did accept the Seebohm recommendations and the Local Authority Social Services Act was passed through Parliament in 1970. This Act ended the Children's Departments (and also of course the Association of Children's Officers and the Association of Child Care Officers). On its demise, the ACCO published a pretty "Souvenir Portrait" booklet bound in silver card. Lucy was among the contributors, with a piece entitled "A Children's Officer Looks at the ACCO". She speaks of the "deep, far-reaching and significant changes" in the field of social development in the twentieth century, in which the ACCO had played a significant part.

> And so another era starts. Just as in 1948 Child Care staff and Children's Officers set out to build a new service using what was sound in the experiences of the past; so the Association of Child Care Officers, in merging with the British Association of Social Workers, will be using the wisdom and experience of the past 21 years and will help in the creation of a new service which will be of significance in the present and a firm foundation for the future.[154]

Seebohm had envisaged a new Director of Social Services to be:

> An effective administrator, the leader of a group of people

with widely differing backgrounds, able to take a broad and informed view of the needs the service ought to be meeting and capable of looking outwards, well beyond the limits of his [*sic*] own department and authority and well into the future.[155]

Again Lucy fitted the bill admirably, except that she was not a he. There was cut-throat competition across the country for these jobs, with female Children's Officers pitted against invariably male Chief Welfare officers in the same authority. Eileen Younghusband called it "a harsh game of musical chairs."[156] Of the 174 Directors appointed, only 21 were women. This was an indication of the ambivalence still felt by councillors about Children's Officers, who were often very able professional women.

This ambivalence did not, however, apply in Oxford. Lucy was formally appointed as Director of Social Services for the City in January 1971. She held the post until 1974, a period during which, according to the *Oxford Mail*, the department was known as "The Lucy Show" after a then popular American TV sitcom.

Much as Lucy would have liked Jenny Fells to stay on as her deputy, she realised that this was politically unacceptable. The Welfare Officer was one Mr Davenport who was not well regarded. (Stella de Gruchy tells a cruel joke from the time, which illustrates the lack of respect for him in the city. "Davenport fell into a hole in the pavement, and two questions arose: one, who pushed him? and two, is he still down there?"). However, Lucy felt duty bound to appoint Davenport as her deputy, as to appoint Jenny would have seemed like a Children's Department takeover. Typically she managed to avoid upsetting Jenny about this, taking the trouble to explain carefully to her exactly what she was doing and why.

Barbara Kahan had been in favour of the Seebohm changes, and had written much of the evidence submitted to the Seebohm Committee by the Association of Children's Officers. Even though her enormous success as Children's Officer for Oxfordshire would have seemed to make her the natural choice for Director of Social

Services for the county, her forceful personality had led to her having made some enemies in the authority. She revealed to Bob Holman, "The Clerk of the Council indicated that, while I was highly regarded, I spent too much money and was unlikely to be appointed".[157] She therefore left the Oxfordshire stage to become deputy chief inspector of children's services at the Home Office, and an influential writer and campaigner on children's issues. Lucy was later to lock horns with her again at the National Children's Bureau of which Kahan was the powerful chair between 1985 and 1994.[158]

To prepare her for her new role, the city council sent Lucy on a two-month full-time management training course at the Institute of Local Government Studies run by Professor Stewart at her familiar Birmingham University. She later said that she had learned from Professor Stewart the basic lesson that "for good administration one must have clear lines of management and that it must be clear exactly who is responsible for what". Perhaps she took the opportunity to look up friends from her Settlement days. She told Abrams:

> I realised that being a Director of Social Services one was going to be much more a manager and much less involved with the staff, with the children, and that one would devolve responsibility to people without oneself carrying it, […] what you had to do was to see that the Department was so organised that the work was done.

She likened the change from Children's Officer to Director of Social Services to moving from running a little local shop where you'd know what was on every shelf, know every customer, and know the few assistants you've got, to running a big supermarket.

Staff coming together from the different parts of the authority had differing levels of enthusiasm for their new, and often very different, roles. Many found adapting difficult, and said so. There were lots of complaints. Hospital social workers perhaps found the changes less daunting, as they were already used to working in a generic way.

Lucy was committed to the further training of her staff. Jenny Fells was sent on the same management course at Birmingham, and she remembers going through with Lucy the possibilities of training for the newly 'genericised' staff. Children's workers had to learn how to implement the 1959 Mental Health Act, a task many of them found challenging, and welfare staff had to learn how to support children. Seebohm had thought that by joining the Social Services Departments, community mental health services would be improved. This proved to be over-optimistic, and the extent of improvement tended to depend upon the enthusiasm of the individual Director.[159] Prior to 1970, Mental Welfare Officers (MWOs) had been employed in the offices of the local Authorities' Medical Officers of Health. They tended to be either ex-nurses or ex-servicemen, and only eighteen per cent were qualified. At the same time, the whole field of Psychiatry was in turmoil as staff were being schooled at university courses where the 'anti-psychiatry' ideas of R.D. Laing and David Cooper held sway. Social workers in the new generic departments became MWOs with often inadequate training.

The new management culture had only a certain impact on Lucy. She still ploughed her own furrow as much as possible. On one occasion, Leicester University sent a gentleman in a suit from their new management course. He was interested in forecasting. He invited Lucy and Jenny to lunch at the Randolph Hotel, sat down with his smart new computer equipment and questioned Lucy about numbers of children in care. He studied the trend over about five years, and confidently came up with a prediction that, in year so and so, that certain number of children would be in care. Lucy looked him in the eye and said, "Oh no, that's not going to happen". "Why not?" "Because I wouldn't let it happen", came the retort.

Oxford City Social Services divided the city into three areas, working generically with all client groups. The area teams were located in City Chambers in Queen Street, whereas Lucy and her administration section were in the headquarters at 77, George Street. Even though they were both in the centre of the small city, the psychological gap between the two was huge. "There was a real us and them feel", says Brand.

One of the three Area Directors was Ruth Evans, who had been in the Family Casework section, and who later went on to write one of the few books by social workers telling the stories of some of the families with whom she worked.[160] In an epilogue, Evans writes about the effects of the Seebohm changes on her personally, and I think her experiences chime with those of Lucy.

> We went into the brave new world of the reorganised Social Services Departments with our flags of hope flying high […] With many others I was sent on a training course for Organisation and Management […] It was informative and enjoyable to meet with colleagues from other disciplines; the mental health and welfare officers. There had been much duplication and overlapping of work, not always fully realised or acknowledged, as was an un-doubted, and not always justified, pride in being specialists. The pooling of resources occupied much of our time during the first year after the reorganisation, and because the time spent on learning new methods of work with new groups of clients vied precariously with daily caseload management; job-satisfaction faltered and declined for a while.

She goes on to describe the differences between work as a child care officer and as a generic social worker:

> When I was a child care officer I had been allowed [by Lucy] to conduct my work in an uncurtailed and unrestricted fashion, time was at my disposal and my discretion. We all worked overtime, perhaps even more unrecorded hours than the now strictly recorded and paid ones. […] The families under supervision were visited several times a week, sometimes, daily, a luxury which cannot possibly be approved of these days. […] I had time to watch developments, to make unhurried decisions, to

wait, when a situation asked for delay, without losing sight of the ultimate aim in a welter of extraneous duties." [161]

Her dissatisfaction at the new state of affairs led her to leave her job as Area Director after only two years.

The two other Area Directors were Kitty Lee and Peter Walkington, both of whom came from Buckinghamshire. Under them there were two team leaders for each area. Don Brand became one of the team leaders under Kitty Lee. Teams were made up of ten or eleven social workers and (unqualified) social work assistants. Teams were expected to make links with the communities in their local areas, called 'patches', and each worker took a mix of clients in their caseloads. One team covered Blackbird Leys and Cowley, one covered Headington and North Oxford, and the third Iffley and East, South and Central Oxford. This pattern of area organisation was replicated in Social Services departments across the country.

At her very first Social Services Committee meeting on 5th January 1971, Lucy got to grips with the new responsibilities for the wider client group. She presented a full report on the implementation of the newly passed Chronically Sick and Disabled Persons Act 1970 (CSDPA), reviewing existing services, identifying gaps in service, and requesting £3,850 for the appointment of a specialist social worker for the physically disabled, and a new permanent post of mental health social worker. She further bombarded councillors with a twenty-six-page report[162] summarising the services being provided and the legislation they were responsible for implementing. There were two full-time home help organisers supporting sixty-three home helps, whose number had doubled over the previous ten years (under the NHS Act 1946). There was a need for major expansion of the meals on wheels service (under the National Assistance Act of 1948). St Nicholas House, Minchery Farm, Littlemore, was a home for twenty mentally handicapped children, and Eastfield House at Brasenose Driftway, Cowley, accommodated twenty-five mentally handicapped adults (under the Mental Health Act 1959). She boasted that the sheltered workshop in Oxford "leads the country in the productivity and economical race" and was involved in a process of 'industrialisation', (under the Disabled Persons Employment Act 1958).

Almost immediately, the provisions of the Chronically Sick and Disabled Persons Act caused Lucy and her committee enormous headaches. On 17 March 1971, the BBC Radio Four *Today* programme, presented at that time by Jack de Manio, reported allegations that Oxford had reduced the amount spent on the chronically sick and disabled between 1967 and 1970 from £12,500 to £2,400. Worse, there were questions asked in Parliament, and Lucy had to appear on the TV programme *Westminster Today* of Saturday 22 May to deal with allegations by a Mr and Mrs Wright that they had not been given a telephone under the terms of the Act. They made no mention of other help that had been given to them by Oxford Social Services. Another complainant was a Miss Nelson, who, as Lucy pointed out, did not even live in the City, but in neighbouring Berkshire. For her Committee Lucy analysed the figures and showed that Oxford's overall welfare expenditure was well above average. She had already recommended that a research student under the supervision of Olive Stevenson of the University Social Work course, Barnett House, do a survey to prepare a full register of disabled people in the City, as required by the CSDPA.[163] A few months later, after she had made further reports to the committee on services to the handicapped, she concludes, "To summarise, while no claim is made that the services are all that one would desire, Oxford has a record of steady development".[164] This has a defensive ring. She warned she would need funding to employ more staff to implement the Act, after "numerous complaints made by various organisations, colleagues and the public". Lucy was struggling with unfamiliar issues and not enjoying it much. Barbara Kahan's social workers in neighbouring Oxfordshire looked on, and some felt themselves to be superior to the City staff after the Seebohm changes. They remained 'Barbara's people' even after Kahan left, and many felt that Lucy was losing her touch.

One of the organisations that had made complaints was the Oxford Disablement Income Group (DIG), which became a powerful pressure group, even at one time requesting representation on the Social Services Committee. Instead, characteristically, Lucy arranged a personal meeting with Dr Bithell, their Chairman. She admitted to him that the reorganisation of the Department had prevented cases being

> dealt with as expediently as they might have been, and indeed some applications for telephones had been overlooked […] If however the DIG carry out a 'war' upon the Social Services this will be of no encouragement to staff who are working under severe pressure and who are anxious and willing to give the handicapped a good service.[165]

Whether this softened the attitude of the DIG is unrecorded.

Another issue that soon became high profile in the new Department was the plight of homeless families. In Oxford, student and tourist demand meant there was very little accommodation available for local families unable to buy a house or flat. As there was a danger of children having to come into care if their parents were evicted for non-payment of rent, there was pressure to bail out the family with 'Section 1' money, a limited budget under the Children and Young Persons Act designed for emergencies only, which soon became exhausted. Lucy was constantly petitioning her committee to negotiate with the housing committee to allocate often sub-standard houses in run-down parts of the city like St Clements to families which, "For the children's sake should not be broken up, but where the parents are incapable of paying rent, due often to mental disturbance".

There was also a very active support group that operated around the Simon Community house for homeless individuals. The Simon Community workers were seen as a great resource by the social workers. Jenny Fells told me of one of her cases:

> I had a very bolshie adolescent in care, very intelligent,

who was causing absolute chaos; nobody could really contain her – her own family couldn't and certainly the children's home couldn't. And then she suddenly found a place for herself; she went along to the Simon Community and worked as one of their helpers. Of course, everyone got most excited, most unhappy about it, but it worked out brilliantly.

Homeless families would arrive at the Social Services office supported by a Simon Community worker, and demonstrations or sit-ins would be staged if social workers were unable to find somewhere for that family – an often impossible task given the lack of housing provision. Brand and some colleagues wrote an open letter to the local paper to raise the issue. "Lucy hauled us in and gently told us off for doing that without letting her know. She said she wouldn't have stopped us doing it, but she needed to know", Brand told me. However, constructively, when the Social Services Committee received a report on the issue, Lucy arranged for the group of staff to address the Committee in person with their concerns.

Under Lucy's Directorship, a residential family centre with space for eight families who needed intensive support to work on their problems was set up. She regarded this centre as one of her main achievements as Director. These centres are notoriously difficult to sustain. While in the unit, problems can be addressed, but families often become over-dependent on the staff, which produces a different set of problems. Another difficulty is that council tenancies are at risk when a family is absent for many weeks. However, this is how Lucy spoke of the centre to Abrams:

> One of the things that I'm terribly sad has gone, but which I think was very good, I did start up a completely new family centre in Oxford, up at Cowley, where we had seven flats and a warden and his wife. And these were for particularly difficult families that we wanted to keep together, but that we felt that both parents needed support. And I regret very much that that's closed now, because

when I was Director of Social Services it was a splendid place.[166]

The situation Lucy inherited in the City's old people's homes sounds dire. A report she presented to the Committee in January 1972 speaks of increasingly frail residents, a deluge of incontinence, and inadequate staffing levels with long hours of overtime and a high sickness rate. She recommended the creation of five posts of Assistant Matron, one in each of the City's homes.

Lucy described to Abrams her understanding of the development of services for elderly people over the years during which she was involved in their care.

> Under the old Poor Law acts, old people were cared for in Public Assistance institutions, and they were enormous places, with sort of 50 sleeping in a dormitory. And we all worked to get rid of the Poor Law institutions, and [...] we did it in steps; first of all we started old people's homes, and then as the years went by, we worked towards keeping old people in the community, which of course is what the concept is now. So that there were really the three stages, [first] when they were in the Poor Law institutions, then [...] they were in either wardened accommodation in their community, or living with their families, [...] and then finally making it possible for them to live in their own homes, by providing meals on wheels, home helps, voluntary visitors, and so on. So you see there's been a significant degree of change over the last twenty years.[167]

Perhaps in an attempt to keep in touch with her social workers, Lucy instituted fortnightly meetings with all the professional staff. Most of the business was routine, but Brand told me how she would also report back on meetings she had had with the Home Office or the Department of Education. She loved name-dropping, and would come back and tell everyone what she had said to Sir Keith Joseph, or the advice she had given to Richard Crossman, or what Jim Callaghan thought of this, that or the other.

An indication of the level of Lucy's concern for her staff comes in a request she put to her Committee in March 1972 for some paid leave for Mrs Stacey, the Matron of Maltfield House children's home, who suffered from asthma. She tells the Committee that Dr Ounsted considers her work of high calibre, and continues:

> The committee will recall that Mrs Stacey received national recognition for her services to child care when she was awarded the British Empire Medal in May 1969. She is a very self-effacing person and did not find the publicity which this entailed very easy to cope with, but those of us who have worked with her felt very proud on her behalf.

What committee member could resist a request couched in such terms?

Apart from her formal use of "Mr" or "Miss" to address staff, Lucy's management style was informal and relaxed. However, staff relations were not all sweetness and light. In March 1972, a group of social work staff, including Don Brand, requested that they receive additional leave in recognition of overtime they worked, (Lucy did frequently report to committee on the overwhelming volume of work and the long hours put in by her social workers) and payment for "stand-by" duty, what would now be called "emergency duty", providing cover for issues that arise out of office hours. The staff were so infuriated by lack of progress on this, and by a letter from Lucy in which she seemed to confuse the two issues, offering them "seven days' extra leave in lieu of stand-by duty", that they wrote directly to the Committee in September of that year renewing their demands. These were subsequently refused by the Establishment Committee.[168]

Meanwhile, international events were having an impact on Oxford. Idi Amin, the Ugandan military ruler, told the country's thousands of Asians to leave the country before November 1972. About thirty thousand of them arrived in England, frightened about the future and leaving their wealth and businesses behind.

The majority landed up in Leicester, but a small number arrived in Oxford, and Lucy, as a Chief Officer, was given responsibility to house and rehabilitate them. As Lucy later told the House of Lords, she found a creative way to meet their immediate needs for shelter:

> The local authority said it could not give them council houses. I then went to Oxfam and posed my problem. At the drop of a hat and without any more ado the then director of Oxfam gave me a cheque for £10,000. With that I bought a house in which I put one family. I then mortgaged that house to buy a second house. In the end I bought fifteen houses with that £10,000.[169]

From about the Autumn of 1972, the volume of work Lucy and her committee were dealing with was huge. At each meeting she presented reports on a whole raft of developments in the Department's work, from providing transport and laundry services, through holiday play-schemes under Urban Aid, to the development of 'Intermediate Treatment' for young delinquents under the Children and Young Persons Act 1969.[170] New residential homes were projected, new office accommodation proposed, new sheltered workshops suggested, and new staff requested – all needing detailed project briefings and financial estimates. It is exhausting just reading about it. There were endless problems at homeless families' accommodation; the Oxford Council of Social Service, chaired by Olive Stevenson, put constant pressure on the Department for grant aid, and, to make matters worse, the fuel crisis of the winter of 1972–73 meant Lucy had to appoint an advice worker and set up temporary accommodation in church halls. The pressure must have been non-stop.

Alongside all this, she was active in the Association of Directors of Social Services (ADSS), although not to the same extent as she had been in the ACO when she was Children's Officer. This Association was set up in 1971 very soon after most Directors were appointed. They initially met in Nottingham to decide what kind of association they should have. Lucy took part in this as she had so recently been President of the ACO. Soon, sub-committees

Lucy Faithfull: mother to hundreds

developed for children, for disability, for older people – the old divisions. This was because there was a real fear that specialist expertise with the different client groups would be lost.

As Director, Lucy was always conscious of her debt to her social workers. When she was awarded the OBE in 1972 she threw a celebratory party for the staff. Brand remembers her speech, in which she acknowledged the work of the department. She smiled, "My dears, I know what people say about the OBE, it stands for Other Buggers' Efforts!" Her investiture at Buckingham Palace was on 22nd February, and a photo taken on the day shows her outside the railings in a smart fur coat accompanied by her rather worried-

Lucy Faithfull and her brother Leigh after her investiture

looking brother in his owlish spectacles. Her Oxford friend, Anna Toulmin, was her second guest.

For many of the staff who worked with Lucy during her sixteen years at Oxford City, this was a golden period in their careers. They pay tribute to her unfailing support of them, her integrity, her courage, her political skills, and her clarity of vision about what she wanted the department to achieve. "She could tolerate the 'unsafe', she wasn't frightened", says Stella de Gruchy. "She gave me the courage to take risks", adds Jenny Fells. "I did gain in confidence under her, she never undermined you. She was never stumped, you could always go to her with a problem, and when you came out you'd be clearer about it".[171] Don Brand, who was moving from Oxford to Kent County Council, wrote that he had felt "cherished", and commented on how important that was in the face of the stress and constant change. It was bearable, he said, "because you obviously cared about the staff and the service". [172]

Nevertheless, many people who knew Lucy in Oxford admit that she was not as eminent a Director of Social Services as she had been as Children's Officer before 1970. The honours that were heaped upon her in the next few years were earned perhaps more by her work between 1958 and 1970 than between 1971 and 1974.

Town and gown are notoriously opposed in Oxford. Lucy was pre-eminently a person representing the former, but, in 1973, 'gown' made her an offer she could not refuse. Sir Alan Bullock, Master of St Catherine's College, decided that she should be offered an Honorary Master of Arts degree. He tells her, "There was no suggestion in my time as Vice-Chancellor which I was happier to put forward, and none which met with such widespread acclaim!"[173] Always modest, if not ashamed, of her lack of formal academic qualifications, Lucy was utterly delighted. In her letter thanking Bullock Lucy writes, "you may be amused to hear that one of our boys said, 'We thought you were good, Miss, but we didn't know you were clever!'"[174] The degree ceremony involved an oration in Latin by her proposer, which paraphrased, included the comment, "On behalf of young children abandoned without hope and other victims of maltreatment, she has stood forth as the doughtiest of champions." After the ceremony, at the Sheldonian Theatre, Lucy gave a celebratory party at *The Bear*, Woodstock.

In 1974, (the year of lethal IRA bombings, the three-day week, and, on the other side of the Atlantic, Watergate), as the monetarist ideas of Milton Friedman and Keith Joseph became increasingly influential amongst politicians, and public spending became a dirty word, yet another reorganisation of local government was taking place. A uniform two-tier structure was introduced, abolishing single-tier areas such as county boroughs. This meant that Oxford City was no longer an independent authority, and all social services were to be provided by the County of Oxford. Lucy, I imagine with some relief, decided that this was the moment to retire from the Social Services Directorship of Oxford City Council. She was sixty-four. Photos taken in Oxford Town Hall at her leaving party, that important rite of passage, show her looking, despite her festive ruffled and diaphanous blue dress, sombre and unsmiling. Valedictory speeches were made by a spectacularly ugly Chair of committee, and she was given, along with a cheque and large bouquet, a portable typewriter, perhaps because Councillors and her staff had battled too long to decipher her incomprehensible handwriting. In her speech she made two wishes: that there should be equality between residential and field social workers, and that social workers could make a successful career without having to move into managerial roles.

She outlined her retirement plans to Drew Clode,

> When I retired from Oxford, I absolutely loved it. I had my whole retirement planned out. My brother and I were going to travel, I was going to bird watch more, which I'm very keen on and never had time to do. I was going to live in France to brush up my French and because I like the French. I knew exactly what I was going to do.[175]

She told Abrams that she had decided she wanted to go on living in Oxford, but that it was not fair to be in Oxford when her successor took over, and so she took the opportunity to revisit her childhood haunts in South Africa, travelling with a friend from that country between May to September of that year. She flew to Johannesburg and from there took the Blue Train down to Cape Town. The next trip was travelling the Garden Route all round the South East Coast of Africa. Next she stayed on a tobacco plantation in Rhodesia, as it was then. In a long letter to Don Brand, one of her Oxford child care officers, she reveals how troubled she is by a South Africa in the grip of apartheid and Rhodesia in turmoil immediately prior to independence. She desperately wanted Africans and Europeans to coexist in peace:

> The country is breathtaking in its vastness and its beauty. I stayed in Cape Town, which must be one of the most wonderful cities in the world. I went to Grahamstown where a dinner party was given for me, attended by Professors of Rhodes University. I sat next to a man who said, 'I have a niece in Oxford who adopted two boys.' I said, 'Yes, I placed them with her.' I went to the Transki [sic] which is being taken over by Africans. I stayed on Coronation Mine in the Witwatersrand area. I felt a real sense of bewilderment and distress; the Europeans are so very kind and nice but the apartheid policy is frightening. At the same time, the Europeans do an enormous amount with and for both the Bantu (Africans) and the Coloureds (multi-racial or Indian or anything else). The government has just closed down a Mission and a hospital run by the Mirfield fathers. The fact remains that as yet the Africans cannot administer in a European way.

> I went to Rhodesia. I stayed in Salisbury, attended Parliament and heard Smith speak. I was taken round the Townships by Father Rogers and Janet Priest and heard of the School of Social Work. The Townships in Salisbury are far better than anything I saw in S. Africa and preferable to many of our Housing Estates.

I lectured at the University, which, unlike South Africa, was multi-racial.

I visited an agricultural show in a Tribal Trust land where the Chiefs, their wives and headmen and Europeans ate and drank together. Then I stayed on a tobacco farm in the north east where the terrorists were operating. The country was lovely, the situation horrible. I am appalled that the World Council of Churches, our own Government and United Nations have, in the past, condoned terrorist activities of a peculiarly horrid nature on the indigenous African country people. I went to a beautiful art show in Salisbury by both African and European artists and attended by black and white people.

Rhodesia has done and is doing far more towards ordered peaceful coexistence than S. Africa and many Africans come to Rhodesia to work from Zambia – Malawi – Mozambique – because conditions for Africans are so good. There is a lot which is wrong in Rhodesia but it is far in advance of S. Africa in liberal ideas.[176]

I then came back, by which time I hoped everybody had forgotten about me!

This was highly unlikely because her successor as Director of Oxfordshire Social Services was John Llewellyn, who had hardly endeared himself to his workers by walking into their office, barely acknowledging them, and starting an audit of the chairs and tables. The difference between his style and Lucy's could hardly have been greater. There was a push to have Jenny Fells continue as his deputy, which would have been fair, and politic in the way Lucy was politic after Seebohm; but no, he appointed the former deputy chief probation officer. The male takeover was complete.

On her return from South Africa and Rhodesia, Lucy had her "inglorious bunions" removed and rejoiced that she could walk again without pain. She then spent months organising the conversion of her large North Oxford house into two flats. Having the builders in was a new experience for her. "I learned of the incredible inefficiency of the building trade and yet how very nice were all the men." She took up residence in the top half of the house, letting the ground floor to visiting academic families. Unlike most Oxford landladies, she loved welcoming babies and young children into her house.

Before Lucy could take up her binoculars to study birds in earnest, she was taken seriously ill with a blockage in her intestine. She always made very light of this episode, but it was in fact colon cancer. She knew that something was wrong and immediately went to the doctor and got it sorted out straight away. Her GP referred her to the surgeon, Malcolm Gough, who swiftly operated on her in July 1975. She did later tell Jenny Fells about it in uncharacteristically graphic detail. "It was awful, they put me in this lovely clean bed, and I messed all over it. I made a shocking mess all over their clean sheets, and they were so nice about it". She was ill for about two months. She made a complete recovery and had no recurrence of the cancer, perhaps because she acted so swiftly and decisively in the first place. She reports to Don Brand a remarkably accurate prediction. "The surgeon says I am so fit that I shall have another 20 years".[177] Gough and his wife Sheila subsequently became very close friends. Unsurprisingly, this busy surgeon at the Radcliffe Infirmary did not become personal friends with many people upon whom he operated, but "Lucy was exceptional, with her great gift for listening, she always made you feel that you were important to her; she was amazingly engaging", he says.

She had yet another retirement project which she explained to Drew Clode.

> I was going to revitalise and reorganise the Sunday School movement because I'm very keen on the Church of England, and […] I think children should learn from their church what are the principles of Christianity. I think this

Lucy Faithfull: mother to hundreds

is very difficult to be taught in school. I had hoped to start a Centre for the training of Sunday School teachers. You see, all the other religions, the Jews, the Muslims, teach their children in their church, but not in the Church of England. I believe it should.[178]

This was one idea she was never to have time to put into action. "It would take a long time. I would have to live to 150 if I were to do that," she said to Drew Clode.

In the same letter to Don Brand Lucy reflects on retirement.

One has time to think and be. I was always sorry that when one was working there did not seem time to read, meditate and be more deeply aware – perhaps if one had not been 'cumbered about with much doing' one might have been more effective.

This gives a glimpse of the spiritual as well as the active sides to Lucy's character, but, nevertheless, she soon set about filling her retirement with a plethora of constructive activities, leaving, I suspect, very little time for meditation. She became Governor of the College of Further Education in Oxford where she hoped to introduce an educational programme for child minders. She was on the Standing Committee of the Residential Care Association,[179] working with Derek Newman on improving the terms and conditions of employment for residential social workers.

She worked for a raft of voluntary organisations. Her friend Phillida Sawbridge, the very active head of the Adoption Resource Exchange (ARE),[180] which worked to place disabled and multi-racial children in permanent families, invited Lucy to become its chair in 1974. Anna Martin was the representative of the Independent Adoption Society at the ARE meetings and conferences, and she found Lucy, "twinkling, matey, lively, charming and very human as chair." The ARE would vet agencies applying to become members of the Exchange, and Lucy used to travel around visiting these applicants. A big issue at the time was whether it was appropriate for single women to adopt. Lucy was very supportive of this idea. (The idea of gay men being able to adopt was not even on the radar at that time.)

Alongside her passion for maintaining children in their own families wherever possible, therapeutic residential care for highly emotionally disturbed children had been a life-long interest of Lucy's. The Caldecott Foundation was (and is) one such therapeutic community. She had got to know James King, Director of Caldecott, while she was a Children's Officer in Oxford. In 1967, as a promising young residential worker without a social work qualification, he had been sent by Leila Rendel, the charismatic founder of Caldecott, on a four-month stint in Oxford Children's Department to gain some experience. During that time he'd come to have a very high regard for Lucy and the way she ran her department. Not long after he became a co-director of Caldecott, several of the existing group of Trustees, then called Councillors, had died and King undertook the task of locating a new group of councillors. He met the now retired Lucy by chance in Heal's store in Tottenham Court Road, took her for coffee, and asked whether she would honour Caldecott by joining the Council.

The Foundation was housed in the stately Robert Adam house leased from Lord Brabourne and his wife, Lady Pamela Mountbatten, at Merstham-le-Hatch in Kent, surrounded by acres of beautiful parkland. Lord Brabourne had been chair of the Trustees, but there was perhaps some difficulty in combining the role of Landlord with that of Chair of Trustees. His deputy was Simon Rodway, Director of Social Services for the Borough of Merton. Rodway had worked at Caldecott for 13 years as a house father, and did expect to become chair when Lord Brabourne resigned, but when Lucy became Chair he was delighted, and worked happily with her. They became close friends. "She threw her weight behind everything she did", Rodway says. James King says the role of the Trustees was as a 'think tank'; any problems were reported to them, and possible solutions discussed. The Council linked the community to the outside world, took care of the finances, and provided an element of external scrutiny to the daily life of the community. Meetings took place every two months, "All the Councillors were incredibly loyal, and Lucy attended every single meeting, and however early we were, she was always there before us," says King. "She was dynamic, forceful with a light touch, but clearly it was hard to say 'no' to her". She was never backward in persuading influential people with money to visit and others to support Caldecott. King felt wonderfully well supported by his Council. "I could ring at any time for advice from experts in most fields – psychiatry, education, law, finance". As the council grew, various sub-committees were formed. Lucy served on the child care committee which she chaired, and was also tireless in her work on the fund-raising committee, particularly for a plan which was dear to her heart, to set up a national college for the training of residential social workers in a building on The Paddocks site. To finance this, and also to finance the building of the new school, residential buildings and a gymnasium to replace the eighteenth-century house (which had served Caldecott well for 60 years, but could be adapted no further), the so-called Hope Appeal was set up, with Sir Evelyn de Rothschild, the banker, as Chair, brought in by Lord Brabourne. Lucy and Sir Evelyn formed a "very special relationship" says King. Richard Attenborough, surprisingly, was also among the Hope Appeal group. (Lucy did try to get an accountant friend of hers, Stuart Holden, involved, submitting his CV to the board At first, all went well between him and Lord Brabourne, but Rodway soon began to feel that Holden was not of the necessary calibre, and his services were dispensed with as soon as Lucy died.) The Paddocks opened in 1992, and put on in-service training courses for Caldecott staff and Kent social workers, which were highly successful but, to Lucy's chagrin, did not make money. The college scheme never really took off, and has now ended.

Lucy had a desire to demonstrate the value of therapeutic residential care of emotionally damaged children at a time when fostering was thought to provide the best form of alternative placement for children in care. She had links with Spencer Milham of the Dartington Research Unit, in Devon, who asked Michael

Little of the Unit to research and write a study of Caldecott, entitled *A Life Without Problems?*[181] This is not an altogether successful book, awkwardly mixing an academic concern to evaluate the outcomes of the therapeutic work with an account of the experience of one abused girl who lived at Caldecott during the research period.

Bessels Leigh was (and is) a residential school near Abingdon for what were, in Lucy's day, called 'maladjusted' boys. Lucy served on the governing body for many years, starting during her years as Children's Officer. She was friendly with the then Headmaster, Stuart Brindley, and it could be that he recruited her, or she might have represented the Children's Department on the board of governors. Judge Quentin Campbell, who was, for many years, the Chair of Governors, reports that not only did she hardly ever miss a governors' meeting, she was also an enthusiastic attendee of school events like carol concerts and sports days. She left the board, Campbell thinks, in about 1994, nominally because she was so busy with her House of Lords commitments, but her leaving may not be unconnected with the fact that Barbara Kahan joined the Board at about that time, and became Chair. One of the things Lucy gossiped to Simon Rodway about was how Barbara Kahan upset the Bessels Leigh staff. Campbell comments on their very different styles; Barbara would confront people head on, whereas Lucy, always looking for the middle way, was adept at handling difficult governors, often with a wicked twinkle in her eye.

She was also appointed to the Council of Dr Barnardo's.[182] She served on the Council (i.e. the board of Trustees) from 1975–85. She felt that social work courses did not put enough emphasis on child care training, and used her influence to encourage Barnardo's specifically to put this in place, not only for their own staff but also for local authority social workers who felt the lack of specific knowledge about the needs of children in their 'generic' work settings. Speaking of her long connection with the organisation, her obituary in *Barnardo's News*, in May 1996 says:

> Throughout her working life, Lady Faithfull had contact

with Barnardo's and said she 'had learned much about child care' from her visits to Barnardo's homes and nurseries when she was at the Home office. She was responsible for placing many children into Barnardo's residential homes around Oxford.

She had to retire at the age of seventy-five as council members cannot serve beyond that age, whereupon she was promptly created a vice-president of the charity as a mark of respect for her deep and campaigning interest in children and young people.

The Oxford branch of Barnardo's was set up in 1978 at Lucy's instigation. She initially arranged a meeting with the Lord Mayor of Oxford in his Parlour, involving interested members of the community, including Sheila Gough, Joanna Johnstone and Sheila Ann Wright. These local branches of national charities are effective in the use of volunteers to raise money, and to generate publicity for the cause by organising local events. One high profile event the Oxford branch organised in Lucy's time was a ball at Blenheim Palace, which was attended by Princess Margaret. Lucy became the patron of the branch.

Lucy was President of the Oxfordshire and Berkshire branch of the NSPCC, and in the 1980s, Patron of the national charity, in which capacity she made a speech at the 1985 AGM.[183] Local branches are mainly concerned with organising fund-raising events. Lucy was useful as a figurehead rather than as a hands-on worker, I suspect.

Honorary Fellowships fell into Lucy's lap. One was of the British Paediatric Association, which was founded in 1928. It was predecessor to what is now the Royal College of Paediatrics and Child Health, formed in 1996. The objectives of the Association were to raise the standard of medical care to children, and to advance the education of the public in child health. In 1993 she was also made an Honorary Fellow of the Royal College of Psychiatrists, writing in her acceptance letter about how much she had owed during her career to psychiatrists such as Donald Winnicott.

The Association of County Councils (ACC) was formed in

1974 to represent the views and interests of the county councils of England and Wales. Its activities included conferences, education and training, research, exhibitions, the collection of statistics, providing an information service and library, holding negotiations on pay and conditions of employment, and meeting with government on particular issues. The membership extended to forty-six county councils in England and Wales.[184] Lucy became its vice-president.

She was also a trustee of the Family Nurturing Network of which Canon Brian Mountford's wife, Annette, a Health Visitor, was a founder. This charity promoted models of family behaviour based on the American Bavelock programme.[185] It began as the Oxford Family Skills Development Project, funded initially by the Joseph Rowntree Foundation. It aimed to develop relationship skills among parents and teachers and also in women's prisons, and ran programmes for small groups of parents. It promoted the idea of "emotional intelligence" as a way to help to enhance close relationships and reduce anger and upset. This has now become the "Family Links" charity, still operating in Oxford with Annette Mountford as chief executive.

Following the Conservative Party victory in the 1970 General Election, Margaret Thatcher had entered the Cabinet as Education Secretary. The first measures she introduced gave an indication of things to come; she abolished free school milk for children over the age of seven, and increased the charges for school meals.[186] However, she had got to know, and obviously to admire Lucy Faithfull at a Department of Education committee on "handicapped"[187] children, on which Lucy had sat in her capacity as Director of Social Services for Oxford. It was Mrs Thatcher who wanted Lucy in the House of Lords. In 1974, Harold Wilson became Labour Prime Minister for the second time, on a very small majority, and he was able to allocate a certain number of life peerages to the Conservative Opposition. Mrs Thatcher recommended Lucy Faithfull to him for one of these.

It could also be that an eminent peeress, Lady Janet Young,

ex-chair of Oxford's Children's Committee, and then Education Committee, also played a role. She and Lucy had become close friends, and Lady Young was also a friend of Margaret Thatcher. These things are often arranged through personal contact. Whatever is the truth of the matter, Mrs Thatcher can scarcely have known what a formidable opponent the woman she was about to take into the Conservative ranks would be.

Notes:

[154] Association of Child Care Officers, "Commemorative Report 1949–1970" (London: Oxford House, 1970).

[155] Seebohm Report, para. 618.

[156] Younghusband, (1978), Chap. 16.

[157] Bob Holman, *Champions for Children: The Lives of Modern Child Care Pioneers,* (Bristol: Policy Press, 2001) p. 64.

[158] Despite Kahan's departure, social workers from the Oxfordshire (County) department felt themselves to be superior to the Oxford (City) department. "We were Barbara's people", one of them told me, even after Barbara left.

[159] Roger Hargreaves, "An Opportunity Lost: Local Authorities and Mental Health Social Work 1970–2007". Talk to the Social Work History Network, King's College, London, 4 April 2008.

[160] Ruth Evans, *Happy Families, Recollections of a Career in Social Work.* (London: Peter Owen, 1977).

[161] Evans, p.163.

[162] Minutes of Oxford City Social Services Committee, Oxfordshire Record Office, St Luke's Church, Temple Road, Oxford OX4 2HT.

[163] Committee minutes, 2 June 1971. This proposal came to nothing, and, in the event, Departmental staff had to carry out the survey themselves.

[164] Committee minutes, 1 September 1971.

[165] Committee minutes, 1 March 1972.

[166] Abrams. Tape transcription.

[167] Abrams. Tape transcription.

[168] Committee minutes, 7 February 1973.

[169] HL Deb. (Series 5) 23 June 1986 Vol. 477 c. 59.

[170] This was intended to be 'intermediate' between routine supervision of young people in their own homes and residential care/custody. For more information, see Thorpe et al, *Out of Care: The Community Support of Juvenile Offenders* (London: Allen & Unwin, 1980).

[171] Jenny Fells and Stella de Gruchy, tape transcription of interview, 3 August 2006.

[172] Letter, Don Brand to LF, 17 December 1974.

[173] Letter, Sir Alan Bullock to LF, 3 January 1974.

[174] Letter, LF to Sir Alan Bullock, 31 December 1974.

[175] Drew Clode, transcription of taped interview with LF, 11 October 1994.

[176] Letter, LF to Don Brand, 5 January 1975.

[177] Letter, LF to Don Brand, 25 January 1976.

[178] Drew Clode, transcription of taped interview with LF, 11 October 1994.

[179] The RCA was set up in 1972, after the Seebohm changes, to represent residential social workers. It became the Social Care Association (SCA) in 1985.

[180] ARE was set up by six adoption agencies, three voluntary and three statutory. The office was in Brixton Road. Local authorities referred children to ARE who were 'hard to place', for example children with a disability. ARE maintained a register of placements and recommended adoptive parents, often in distant parts of the country.

[181] Michael Little, *A Life Without Problems? The achievements of a therapeutic community*, (Aldershot: Arena, 1995).

[182] Dr Barnardo's Homes, established in the 1870s, shortened its name to Barnardo's in 1988, reflecting the move away from Victorian-style institutional residential care for children.

[183] Speech at NSPCC AGM at the Queen Elizabeth Hall, 22 May 1985.

[184] The ACC was incorporated into the Local Government Association (LGA) in 1997.

[185] Bavelock, S. *Effective family based approaches to treating and preventing child abuse and neglect.* (Salt Lake City, UT: Family Development Resources Inc., 1990).

[186] Earning her the nickname 'Thatcher, Thatcher, milk snatcher'.

[187] LF tended to use the language of her generation. Now "Children with special needs" is the phrase in use.

CHAPTER SIX

THE LUCY FAITHFULL FOUNDATION

The fact that Lucy not only lent her name but also helped to set up the Lucy Faithfull Foundation shows something of her mettle, because work with sex offenders is not a popular cause. She saw it very much as a child protection concern. She would stand up and be counted on things that mattered to her about children. I think that was really courageous, and is one of the things I admire her most for.[188]

So says Adrianne Jones, who was Director of Social Services for Birmingham while Lucy had that same job in Oxford. At Lucy's invitation, Adrianne now serves on the Trustees of the Lucy Faithfull Foundation.

Lucy joined the House of Lords in 1975. Alongside all the issues with which she was to involve herself there, she had a parallel life trying to protect children by finding ways of working therapeutically with child sexual abusers.

It may have been her experience of the crucial shift in thinking about physical abuse of children in the 1960s that led to her early acceptance of the unpalatable fact that adults could abuse children not only physically, but also sexually. Then, in 1978, she became closely involved in the passing through Parliament of the then highly controversial Protection of Children Act, which makes illegal the making and circulation of indecent pictures of children. (*See Chapter 7.*) Later, during the passage of the Criminal Justice Bill of 1987, Lucy made a strong speech in the House of Lords advocating the admissibility in court of video recordings of interviews with abused children.

> At present the law, as it applies to child witnesses in criminal proceedings, seems to be biased in favour of the molesters. First, the law requires the child or adult to tell her embarrassing story in open court in the presence of the person who is said to have attacked her. As a social worker dealing with such children, I know that there is nothing more distressing to a child than to give evidence against her father in front of a full court. Although a child may have been abused by her father, she nevertheless has a sense of loyalty to him. It is most extraordinary, but the child experiences the most terrible sense of guilt from having to speak against the father in court in an atmosphere the child is not used to.[189]

She went on to explain the system that was indeed later adopted, whereby the recording of an interview with the child is made available to prosecution and defence, and the child need not come into open court. Also, she pointed out, in many cases when the defendant is presented with the video evidence, he pleads guilty, thus preventing the trauma and distress of a full court case. So, back in the 1980s, Lucy not only had a clear grasp of the complex and difficult issues surrounding child sexual abuse, but she also had a way of articulating them in understandable ways to a largely unsympathetic audience.

In the early 1980s, a young Probation Officer and ex-submariner called Ray Wyre was working in Albany Prison on the Isle of Wight with large numbers of men who had been convicted of sexual abuse of children. He had realised, to his consternation, that this group of offenders in general got little or no treatment while they were within the prison system. They often had little or no insight or understanding of the effect on their child victims of their abuse. When they were released, these habitual paedophiles went out into their communities with the same sexual desires, the same attitudes, and the same behaviours that had led them to offend in the first place. He wrote that:

> Sometimes the only way I knew where they were heading was by the destination stamped on the regulation railway warrant handed to them at the gate. The result was dangerous men, often resentful about being punished, with no supervision, a bigger set of paedophile contacts, and no official record of their whereabouts. It was complete madness.[190]

On their release, they were forbidden to live with the family in which they had abused, so they often moved to another part of the country, got jobs, settled down and again started targeting children in the new area and repeating their abusive behaviour.

Some offenders, on the other hand, desperately wanted treatment so that they could return to their own families. Ray Wyre started developing ways of breaking through their denial of guilt, and their blame of the child, helping them to understand the effects of their abuse on children, and to find ways of controlling their behaviour. His rehabilitation regime became recognised as effective for these men, and he quickly became an acknowledged expert in what was then a very specialist field. He was not willing, however, to work meekly within the bureaucratic constraints of a Probation Area, and was often the despair of some of his Hampshire managers. Wyre thought that his treatment system would be more effective on a residential basis, and started looking for a means to develop such a service. He went freelance, and asked his accountant if he knew of "someone with a million pounds" to back him. He was introduced to a Birmingham businessman and property developer whom I shall call Mr P. Mr P. had a suitable property, at 25–29 Park Road, Moseley, Birmingham, and he and Ray Wyre started the Gracewell

Clinic there in 1988. Park Road was at the heart of Birmingham's red light district, and the houses that were to become Gracewell formed a terrace that used to be a casino. Workmen ripped out the chandeliers and red flock wallpaper, built interviewing rooms and installed the state-of-the-art video equipment and one-way mirrors necessary for therapeutic work.

At around the same time, Wyre was asked to speak at a conference in Windsor organised by Elizabeth Sieff.[191] Lucy Faithfull was at the conference and was impressed by Ray Wyre's work and ideas. They had long conversations outside of the formal business of the conference. Wyre thinks that she shared his determined streak, that she was like him in that she also had an impatience with obstructive systems, and a desire to promote work that was demonstrably effective, despite opposition from various quarters. Lucy wrote of this time:

> Ray, together with Hilary Eldridge and Jenny Still, worked out a formula for treating the men. The Judiciary was notified of the work of the Clinic. The Home Office through the Probation Service paid for the men. I spent time at the Clinic and was much impressed by the work being done. I was then asked to be a Trustee.

Elizabeth Sieff was also asked to be a Trustee, as was Diana Lamplugh (who had set up the Suzy Lamplugh Trust in memory of her daughter, the estate agent who disappeared while showing a client around a property). Dr Alan Gilmour of the NSPCC was the fourth trustee. It later turned out that Mr P. had never informed the Charity Commissioners of the appointment of these "trustees". He managed his other business interests, a company called Brodale Ltd, from a house next door to Gracewell.[192]

Wyre describes the work of the clinic. It was a dual-site operation, a hostel and a separate clinic that men attended each day:

> Normally the men would be with us for a year – assuming they lasted the intense four-week assessment period. This stage was crucial, both for them so that they could

begin the long process of confronting and controlling their offending and for us so that we could be sure that Gracewell was the right place to treat them [...]

Once the formalities of each morning's arrivals were completed, the clinic became very quiet. At 10 o'clock, the men divided into three small sets – one set for assessment and two treatment groups run by experienced key workers.

These were trained therapists I had brought to Gracewell from the probation service, social work and other agencies involved with child care or child protection. They would be the most important figures in the men's lives, working with them intensively throughout their year at Gracewell...

Words were teased out of the reluctant, the embarrassed or the defiant; torrents flowed out of others who sought a way to minimise the impact of their offences or to expiate their guilt for the pain they had inflicted on those smaller and weaker than they [...] The basis of our effort was to bring out into the open the things that society refuses to recognise; the needs and influences that drive a man to abuse. Expose them to public view, and society can learn from them and become a safer place; expose them to the man himself, and change becomes a very real possibility. That was what Gracewell existed to achieve.[193]

The treatment programme was divided into five basic modules, addressing firstly the offenders' distorted thinking (for example that the child had been seductive in some way or welcomed the abuse), then victim awareness (helping the men to put themselves in the powerless position of the young child), then teaching them to control their sexual fantasies, training in assertiveness, and teaching about female/male sexuality. Services for the families where abuse had taken place were also developed, particularly by Jenny Still, a social worker who had come to Gracewell from Great Ormond Street Children's Hospital. The Clinic quickly became a centre of excellence in the treatment of sexual abusers, and developed training programmes for other professionals such as probation officers, social workers, and the police. The NSPCC were soon to develop services for sexually abused children and their abusers, but, apart from Gracewell, there were few other sources of advice and expertise for professionals suddenly confronted with these highly controversial and deeply painful issues. The stresses on all the therapeutic staff at Gracewell must have been enormous. The oppressiveness of spending day after day in small rooms filled with child molesters is hard to imagine. Also, abusers are masters of targeting any vulnerability in their helpers.

Gracewell had been registered as a charity in December 1990. In May 1991, with the aim of giving their work some official monitoring and oversight, Gracewell had sought and been granted registration by the Regional Health Authority as a 'nursing home'. That description was not strictly accurate, but the Health Authority, with the blessing of Whitehall, was prepared to be flexible. Official recognition was gained. Police, probation, and the courts, all of which referred men to the clinic, were loud in praise of the programme. Research commissioned by the Home Office as to its effectiveness was in progress. However the local population was not won over. Despite the fact that not a single man had committed further offences while at Gracewell, a small handful of residents began a campaign to force the clinic away from their streets. Wyre describes one frightening episode in the protest campaign:

> Just after we closed our doors one evening in 1992 I heard the sound of an explosion in the porch. There were two of us left in the clinic: the offenders had not been in the building that afternoon, as it was Friday, and the second half of the day was devoted to working with abused children and their mothers. The last had left less than an hour earlier. We ran back downstairs. In the porch we were

greeted by a wall of flames nine feet high. We managed
eventually to extinguish the fire and walked through the
charred woodwork to look outside.

A man was standing watching us. I walked over to him
and asked if he had seen what had happened. Quite calmly
he said he had laid the fire and pointed to an empty petrol
can lying in the bushes near by. I was stunned and asked
him why he had done this, and he said simply, 'There
were perverts in there.' I explained we had only mothers
and children that afternoon and suggested that, as he had
tried to burn us down, he should come and look around
inside. It was the first time he [...] gained any insight into
our work. I gave him a cup of coffee and called the police.
He and I sat together in reception as we waited for the
officers to come and arrest him.[194]

Another trouble was that, over time, Lucy and the other trustees
became concerned that Mr P., who called himself Chief Executive,
was failing to produce annual financial reports, even when formally
requested to do so. She wrote, "I wished to be assured that the
Birmingham City Council was both aware of the work being
done and also approved of the methods used". The City Council
undertook an Independent Review, and their report of June
1992 found that the professional work done by Ray Wyre and
his colleagues was of a high quality, but there was concern over
the financial and administrative arrangements. "The irregularities
in establishing Gracewell as a charity tarnished the image of the
organisation", it said, and recommended that "the enmeshment
between the commercial business and Gracewell be ended". Lucy
asked to meet Mr P. at the House of Lords, and was astonished to
be told by him that she and Elizabeth Sieff and Diana Lamplugh
were no longer trustees; he had appointed others. She was aware
that this was quite against Charity legislation, and immediately
contacted the Charity Commissioners, and she and the other
trustees formally resigned.

Meanwhile, with Ray Wyre so much in demand as an expert, he was often away on speaking engagements and other consultative work. In his absence, Mr P., despite his lack of any relevant qualification, began to put himself forward as a spokesman for Gracewell at professional conferences, causing confusion and frustration among delegates who found his input unhelpful. Hilary Eldridge points out that when an organisation is dependent financially on one wealthy person, and not in receipt of other regular and reliable funding, which was the situation at Gracewell at that time, it is understandable that that person can get anxious and can tend to want to try to do the job themselves. There were also rifts between the staff of Gracewell and Mr P. An excoriating letter from Lucy to P. asking for her name to be withdrawn from Gracewell sums this up,

> The team as I understand it, were concerned that your personal style of management demanded, rather than enlisting [sic] loyalty, which has led to tensions in the personal relationships with the staff [...] You may feel it advisable to withdraw in the very near future.[195]

The staff offered their resignations, whereupon P. did himself resign. Rodney Reed, who had an administrative role at Gracewell, later made a range of allegations against Mr P. in evidence to the Charity Commission's subsequent Section 8 Investigation. However, the finding of the investigation, in the spring of 1994, was that there had been no evidence of financial irregularity.[196]

All this is most unsavoury, and I can only assume that Lucy became aware of the difficulties at a late stage. By her own admission the four trustees met on only three occasions between 1988 and 1990. Ray Wyre suggests that the Lucy initially admired P. for his willingness to put his own money into the Clinic, and was willing to "let him get on with it".

While all this was going on, the North Moseley Residents' Association, led by a local magistrate, was still opposed to Gracewell, fearing that the men might interfere with their children. Lucy writes, "This, as far as I know, has never happened, and their fears were based on apprehension rather than fact. Nevertheless, it has to be said that their fears were perhaps understandable." Local councillors were lobbied, and in the autumn of 1993, Birmingham City Council sent a letter formally withdrawing planning consent. The clinic would have to close. Wyre writes sadly that, on Wednesday 29 December 1993,

> I locked the heavy green door of 25–29 Park Road, Moseley for the last time. The offices were silent, the staff dispersed. The men, offenders all [...] were scattered to the winds [...] Gracewell had been an attempt to protect children by working with men who were determined to abuse them, and now it was all over.

The irony of the closure is that, while the men were at Gracewell, the courts, probation and the local police knew exactly where they were, and their offending behaviour was being addressed. After the closure, they returned to live anonymously in their communities, unsupervised and untreated. As Wyre points out, "By closing Gracewell the council and the residents did not protect one more child. In fact, the reverse is true: they put children at risk."[197] Variations on this "not in my back yard" syndrome were to dog all subsequent efforts to continue residential work with these offenders.

The Home Office research that had been carried out in 1991–2 was finally published in 1994. It was carried out by independent researchers, known as the STEP team (Sex Offenders Treatment Evaluation Project),[198] who took a sample of twenty Gracewell residents and compared their progress in relation to similarly categorised men in non-residential community-based programmes, using pre- and post-treatment measures. The outcome was very positive for the Gracewell programme, but, sadly, publication came too late to influence the decision to close the clinic.

After the departure of Mr P., Lucy, the staff and the other trustees began to look for ways in which this groundbreaking work with sex offenders could be continued in the interest of protecting children. Lucy had spent her entire career committed to children's well-being, and she was not going to be deterred at this point. Accordingly, the Lucy Faithfull Foundation was set up to take over the work of Gracewell, with Lucy as Chairman, and with Elizabeth Sieff and Alan Gilmour continuing their trustee roles. The trustee group was strengthened by the addition of Richard Monk, Assistant Chief Constable for Devon and Cornwall, Superintendent Michael Hames, Head of the Metropolitan Police Obscene Publications Unit at New Scotland Yard, and Frank Cook MP. All Gracewell's assets and files were legally transferred to the new Foundation.

The Trustees heard of a disused Nursing Home in the Bedworth area near Coventry which was owned by Coventry City Council, called the Moat House. The Labour Party in power in Coventry voted to rent the Moat House to the Faithfull Foundation at a rent of £45,000 a year. The staff set about to win hearts and minds, in a spirit of openness, and worked hard to involve the community. They went to public meetings, sent out leaflets, made speeches about the work, talked to the media, and so on, but with only mixed success. Lucy continues:

> When [plans for the Moat House] became known, a protest group formed itself (it is said, but not confirmed that the National Front were behind it). At that time, there were local elections being held and the renting of the Moat House for a Men's Clinic/Hostel for treatment of sex offenders became a political issue: Labour for the project – Conservative against.[199]

Lucy invited several eminent peers, together with Ray Wyre and Rodney Reed, and other people whose support she aimed to enlist in order to continue the work of Gracewell, to a meeting at the House of Lords in June 1992, with the aim of raising money for setting up The Moat House as an alternative residential centre. At another meeting, this time with the City Council at Coventry Town Hall, feelings ran high, the press became involved, and the protestors threatened to burn down the Moat House, whereupon the insurance company immediately withdrew cover. Lucy found this very sinister, and pointed out that the threat of arson might well become the weapon of choice for groups opposed to all kinds of care in the community projects, as they would become un-insurable. The loss of The Moat House led to a considerable gap between the closure of Gracewell and the opening of a new residential centre.

Hilary Eldridge,[200] who had been head of training at Gracewell, told me that, despite the lack of residential hostel, the therapeutic and assessment work continued. Lucy and the trustees asked Hilary to be the Clinical Director of the Foundation. (Ray Wyre was, by this time, looking for more independence, so he became an advisor, rather than staff member.) The training programme continued, from rented offices, as did the integrated family work developed by Jenny Still. This was paid for on a case-by-case basis by Social Services or lawyers for providing reports to the Family Courts. This work involved assessing the abuser, but also working with the children and the non-abusing parent. At the same time, they began to work with young people who sexually abuse other children.

With all the problems involving the Moat House lease, the Trustees and staff decided to try and buy a property of their own. They started to hunt round for new premises in less populated areas, and eventually a large house was found called The Boynes near the village of Upton upon Severn, Worcestershire. Negotiations were entered into for the purchase of this property with the money raised from charities. Again, huge efforts were made to bring the local population on side. Public meetings were held, the local vicar was supportive, and personnel from the local Social Services, Health Authority and church representatives were invited to a conference at the Old Palace, Worcester, in September 1993 entitled, "A Christian Response to the Treatment of Sex Offenders". Despite all this work, there was soon uproar in Upton, with groups from Moseley and Bedworth joining in with local protest meetings, giving exaggerated and distorted stories of the work that would be carried out. Mr. P's questionable business dealings were also often brought up – that sad episode seeming to haunt those fighting for the continuation of the service.

Notices went up in Upton, "NO SEX HOSTEL HERE".

Sometimes the word hostel somehow became erased so that the notice read "NO SEX HERE". Lucy apparently told her friend Simon Rodway that a local doctor put up a sign saying: "Free castrations carried out here."[201] I cannot believe this really happened, it must have been a colourful invention by Lucy, but it does convey the virulence of the opposition she had to face. What is certain is that a hedge was deliberately set on fire at The Boynes, and the threat of yet more arson attacks decided the despairing trustees that there was no alternative but to sell the house.

While The Boynes was on the market, the one insurer who could be found who was willing to provide cover for the property imposed "almost ludicrous levels of security" including twenty-four-hour patrolling guards and the installation of automatic movement-activated lights, temporary fencing with anti-personnel wire, and CCTV. Lucy had the unenviable task of raising funds for this huge and fruitless expense, which she calculated amounted to £32,000. Her pleas to the Home Office, perhaps unsurprisingly, fell on deaf ears. "It is vitally urgent that I see you", she wrote to David Maclean, Minister of State at the Home Office, "over

The Boynes

the unfortunate affairs of the Faithfull Foundation." This request was evidently counter-productive, "The trustees went to see the minister, Mr Maclean, and found him utterly unhelpful, difficult and uncooperative. Indeed, he said that men who had sexually abused their children should be castrated!"[202] A cold letter from Maclean after this bruising encounter reads,

> The appropriate way for the Home Office to be involved is through individual referrals from the probation service when the project is up and running. I understand that local probation services have made considerable use of the services in Birmingham, and if they are satisfied with what you are offering, I have no doubt that they will continue to do so in Upton.[203]

Lucy wrote despairingly to Diana Lamplugh:

> We are having terrible trouble with Gracewell. Gracewell closes today, 29 December [1993], and we have not found an alternative house so the men are going to live in Bail Hostels and going daily to a Salvation Army Hall which we have rented. Meanwhile I raised the money and we bought a house in Upton on Severn which was very suitable, but eventually we gave it up as there was so much trouble in the neighbourhood. Now I am having difficulty selling it! Although I intend to maintain the Faithfull Foundation I am not sure how this is going to happen as at the moment we have not the money.[204]

All this campaigning for treatment for sex offenders was, of course, deeply controversial, not least amongst some of her colleagues in the Lords, who were bemused that she should spend so much effort on behalf of such an unattractive group of people. After her death, Simon Rodway had a condolence letter from one colleague who had expressed sympathy to Lucy about all the opposition she was encountering. Lucy had replied, "Don't worry, I'm used to it. All over the Lords I am being called 'Lady Sex!'"[205]

Lucy was also anxious that, unless alternative accommodation could be found, the skilful staff of Gracewell would find employment elsewhere and their experience and expertise would be lost. Meanwhile, she had, on at least one occasion, received a threatening phone call made to the place she stayed when she was in London, with her friends Stuart and Jilly Holden in Wimbledon. Luckily the Holdens were out, and Hilary Eldridge thinks Lucy would not have told them about it, not wanting to worry them. "Lucy took it very calmly. We were appalled, climbing the wall, but Lucy was perfectly calm," Hilary says.

In the spring of 1994, Lucy was temporarily out of action having cracked her ribs in a fall on the Isle of Wight. Rodney Reed was a key figure in keeping Lucy informed of developments. He joyfully faxed Lucy on 2 March 1994, "We completed the sale of The Boynes today." Later that month he told her that, through her contacts and those of others, he had been able to open discussions with various hospitals and Health Trusts with a view to renting accommodation within a Hospital site. Lucy had been working like mad behind the scenes. Eventually, the Department of Health introduced the Foundation to the Riverside Mental Health Trust, which offered to rent them a redundant nurses' home in the grounds of Horton Hospital in Epsom. This was to be on a short-term basis as the hospital was scheduled for closure. This arrangement would obviously minimise the danger of local people feeling threatened by the presence of the clinic. It remained for Lucy to continue to rush around persuading the Department of Health and the Home Office to fund this new project. She involved Baroness Blatch, who, at that time, was Minister of State at the Home Office. She put down a question in the House of Lords in January 1995 "To ask Her Majesty's Government, in the light of successful treatment of sexual offenders, when the Home Secretary will give a considered reply to his verbal agreement of 4 May 1994 to consider the treatment of family men convicted of sexually abusing children to prevent further offences." Baroness Blatch rather dismissively replied, "We have the application for grant support from the Faithfull Foundation under careful consideration"

Lucy Faithfull: mother to hundreds

but a decision is not expected "for some weeks yet".

Lucy, ever the thoughtful diplomat, and perhaps with an eye to future referrals, wrote to the Chief Probation Officer for Surrey, Michael Varah, alerting him "at this very early stage" of the Foundation's interest in the property at Horton Hospital.[206] Gradually, obstacles were overcome, and a residential programme was set up at Horton Hospital, known as The Wolvercote Clinic, (after Lucy, whose full title was Baroness Faithfull of Wolvercote). Hilary Eldridge was the Clinical Director and Ray Wyre continued as a consultant to the Foundation. Lucy arranged a celebratory reception, (at which no Home Office minister was willing to speak) in the Cholmondley Room at the House of Lords, with its canopied terrace overlooking the Thames, in November 1994. Lucy commented "Democracy sometimes works!" and she went on to attribute the opening of Wolvercote to a mixture of effective practice and political will.[207] It opened in the Spring of 1995. A year later, Lucy died, having succeeded, against all the odds, to set her Foundation on a firm footing.

What was the impetus that led Lucy, by then in her eighties, to involve herself in this unpopular cause? Some of her friends wondered if she had been slightly "hijacked" or at least sidetracked from her core concerns by the sex abuse lobby. But I think she realised that the work of Gracewell resonated very well with the Children Act 1989, which she had been instrumental in steering through the Lords. This held that, when sexual abuse happened within the family, rather than take children into care, it would be better for the man to leave home, so, as Ray Wyre says, "the vision at that time was firstly it would take the men out of the family and do a proper comprehensive assessment, and it would also act as an alternative to custody for men who would serve less than four years."[208] Wyre thinks that when he met Lucy, he used language that she related to. He spoke of the stupidity of rescuing women and children from the river while ignoring the man who had pushed them in; of the foolishness of building hospitals and prisons at the bottom of the cliff instead of putting up a fence at the top.

In her Social Services Director days, he thinks, she had criticisms of the way the system dealt with child protection, and that she felt that, sometimes, children, even if they were in families where they may not be seen as safe, might still be better off than if they were moved into other systems that were also unsafe. This certainly links with her post-evacuation research findings, and also with her work in Oxford Children's Department to keep children in their own homes and prevent them coming into care. It also perhaps harked back to her own childhood experience of having to leave her own family at an early age.

Until recently, when a child disclosed sexual abuse in the family, the consequence, with an absence of any treatment option for the man, was almost invariably that the family was broken up, the child perhaps taken into care and the offender banished. Children who have been sexually abused invariably want the abuse to stop, but they often still love and care about their abuser and they fear that if they tell anyone what is happening, their family will be destroyed. Too often this is what happened. Hilary Eldridge thinks that Lucy had perhaps come across families where sex abuse had happened in her own clinical work. Lucy once talked to Hilary about a case when she was a social worker where she had thought 'this isn't right'. Perhaps it was a particular case that had first engaged her interest.

The residential aspect of Gracewell and Faithfull Foundation provision also related closely to her interests. She believed that therapeutic residential work could meet needs in a way that no other provision could. At the same time that these often traumatic events were happening with the Foundation she was equally intensely involved in efforts to maintain therapeutic communities for emotionally disturbed children, such as the Caldecott Community in Kent. Wyre also says, I think rightly, that she was someone who was willing to put her head above the parapet, to stand up for an unpopular cause, even if it was not a vote-winner, if she felt it to be important to do so.

Up to and after Lucy's death in 1996, the work continued

successfully at Horton Hospital until the Health Authority finally closed the site in 2003. Lucy might turn restlessly in her grave if she knew that, since that time, the Foundation has been unable to find suitable alternative accommodation of its own for residential work with sex offenders, and indeed even in 2009, there is no such provision anywhere in the country. However, she would be delighted that the work of the Foundation does continue, and indeed goes from strength to strength. As Hilary Eldridge says: "You don't just stop. The range of things that we currently do we have developed more, probably, because there wasn't a clinic." The rehabilitation programme for sex offenders that Gracewell and the Faithfull Foundation pioneered has been highly influential in the development of the now standard treatment within the criminal justice and youth justice systems, and their work with child victims and the families of abused children continues.

Having no children of her own, Lucy bequeathed[209] money to the many charities with which she was involved, including the Faithfull Foundation, but her legacy to children and families in trouble was much more than financial. "She would have wanted to be remembered for the positive things, the political will that she employed, the persistence, not just in relation to the Foundation, but in terms of children. She was a fighter for them, she was a terrier; she succeeded and she was enormously effective. She was great, and she did so much for children". So says Hilary Eldridge.

She was indeed, a "Mother to hundreds".

Notes:

[188] Adrianne Jones, Tape transcription of interview, 14 May 2007.
[189] HL Deb. (Series 5) Vol. 489 c. 275, 22 October 1987. *Lords Hansard,* Vol. 489, Col. 275, Oct. 1987.
[190] Ray Wyre and Tim Tate, *The Murder of Childhood.* (London: Penguin, 1995). p. 27.
[191] Widow of the Director of Marks and Spencer and founder of the Michael Sieff Foundation, which organises annual interdisciplinary conferences on child welfare.
[192] Information from a TV programme on Gracewell in the Channel 4

series *Free for all* broadcast on 23 March 1993.

193 Wyre and Tate, p. 2.

194 Wyre and Tate, p. 260.

195 Letter, LF to Mr. P., 27 June 1992.

196 The official record of this investigation has now been destroyed by the Charity Commission.

197 Wyre and Tate, pp. 262–3.

198 Beckett, R., Beech, A., Fisher, D. and Fordham, A.S. (1994) *Community-based Treatment for Sex Offenders: an Evaluation of Seven Treatment Programmes.* London, Home Office Publications Unit.

199 LF, typed document, The Faithfull Foundation: A Registered Charity, 12 July 1993.

200 Hilary Eldridge, with Ray Wyre wrote a chapter describing the Faithfull Foundation treatment programme. It is Eldridge, H.J. and Wyre, R., 'The Lucy Faithfull Foundation Residential Program for Sexual Offenders', in Marshall, W.L. et al. *Sourcebook of Treatment Programs for Sexual Offenders.* (New York: Plenum, 1998).

201 Simon Rodway, tape transcription of interview, 19 July 2005.

202 Letter, LF to Ian Sparks, The Children's Society, 2 January 1994.

203 Letter, David Maclean to LF, 7 Sepember 1993.

204 Letter, LF to Diana Lamplugh, 29 December 1993.

205 Simon Rodway (Caldecott Community), *Reflections on Lucy Faithfull.* Unpublished note.

206 Letter, LF to Michael Varah, 4 May 1994.

207 Hilary Eldridge, tape transcription of interview, 23 July 2007.

208 Ray Wyre, tape transcription of interview, 11 August 2005.

209 "Latest Wills", *The Times*, 2 July 1996.

CHAPTER SEVEN

RELUCTANT PEERESS

For part of her convalescence after her bowel cancer operation back in 1975, Lucy set off for a holiday with a friend to the Irish Republic. It was while she was there that Number Ten was trying to contact her to offer her the peerage. Just at that time, the Irish police were engaged on a huge manhunt, or rather woman-hunt, for members of an IRA gang led by Rose Dugdale, a millionaire's daughter and Oxford graduate turned republican rebel. This group had forced its way into the stately Russborough House, bound and gagged the wealthy owners, Sir Alfred and Lady Beit, and made off with nineteen works of art, including a Vermeer, and paintings by Rubens, Goya and Velasquez.[210] Their aim was to trade the paintings for the release of the Price sisters, who were on hunger strike in prison. There had been other female members of the art-heist gang, and the men in the Gardai were jumpy. When Number Ten (this was still Harold Wilson's premiership) called them in an effort to trace a Lucy Faithfull, there was, apparently, some confusion initially as to who they were looking for, a potential baroness or the harbourer of a republican criminal.[211] "Our remote cottage on the Galway coast was visited by Police as we were strangers, had an Oxford number plate, and I knew Rose Dugdale. Having searched the cottage, the police said that, of course, they knew all the time we were not harbouring them", she tells Don Brand.[212]

However, eventually Mrs Thatcher got through to Lucy with the invitation, catching her off guard. "Oh, how simply awful, it would terrify me out of my wits, and I don't think I'm bright enough to go into the House of Lords", she blurted out. "There was a frightful silence on the other end of the telephone. She simply couldn't believe her ears. She said: 'But don't you realise there are queues waiting to go into the House of Lords?'" 'But Mrs Thatcher,' came Lucy's reply, 'I'm not in the queue'".

She went to the public library and looked through the list of peers and found that there was no Director of Social Services in the House. Indeed there never had been a social worker on the Lords benches.[213] She then phoned her brother Leigh, who told her, in his "drawly solicitor's voice", "If you go into the House of Lords you'll regret it; if you don't go into the House of Lords you'll regret it. So you'd better regret positively rather than negatively!" Leigh was a quiet and unassuming person, who tended not to initiate conversations, and was often to be seen in a soup-stained old jumper, but he was "definitive", in Malcolm Gough's words; he could make decisions. Lucy clearly valued his advice and he was very important to her. So she came to realise that this would be an opportunity to make her professional experience of child care and Social Services effective on a wider stage. So Lucy was initially a reluctant peer, but "Few could have imagined the outstanding, tireless and rebellious advocate that she became", adds Philpot.

She began to ponder what she should call herself. Lady Faithfull of Where? The village of Godstow is just up the Woodstock Road from her house, with its famous pub, the Trout Inn, on the riverbank, setting of many a fictional pint drunk by Colin Dexter's Inspector Morse. One of her ex-clients, on being updated about her thinking, declared, "Oh, no, you can't be 'Godstow', you'd be called the Old Trout!" So she settled for "Wolvercote".[214] Tom White told me frankly:

> I think there was quite a bit of surprise [in the ADSS] when she was elevated to the peerage. If you'd asked

Lucy Faithfull: mother to hundreds

which Director would be given the opportunity to go the House of Lords you wouldn't have said Lucy. If you were looking at Oxford you would have said Barbara [Kahan] because she was very much more prominent than Lucy, though she was a rebel. Then there were the John Chants, the Brian Roycrofts [...][215] Oxford was not seen as the best department in the world, not a leading one. There was perhaps a feeling that it was a shame that we hadn't got someone who was more able, though of course Lucy soon demonstrated how able she really was in very short shrift, but at the point it happened we needed a more prominent advocate of national social work. She was seen as a very good, nice lady. How effective, well, there was some doubt really [...]

As the years went, White admits, there developed nothing but enormous admiration for the way in which she spoke up for social services, and an awareness of how "her very capacity to underplay her ability and knowledge made so many people relate to her and give her the information which allowed her to fire her bullets later".

Lucy's archive contains hundreds of letters of congratulation on her elevation to the peerage from friends, colleagues and from people who used, as children, to be in the Care of Oxford City. In Lucy's letters of acknowledgement, she often writes that she has promised Mrs Thatcher that she will be a working peer. Eileen Younghusband wrote to say, "You will certainly be a Faithfull Lady to the cause of children, as you have been for all the years in the past". "I am awed but absolutely delighted", her local paper, the *Oxford Mail* reports Lucy as saying. She told another friend that some of the Department's delinquent children, now grown up, considered that it was because of them she had been given a peerage, and that they should be allowed to come to the House of Lords with her. "That would be a shock to their Lordships!"[216] "I am to be introduced [to the House of Lords] on 17th February 1976 and Lady Janet Young, who was my Chairman for five years, and

Lord Seebohm, are to be my sponsors",[217] she joyfully writes to a friend. "Bea Serota is lending me her hat", she adds, and it was some hat. These three, Lady Young, Lord Frederick Seebohm and Baroness Beatrice Serota[218] were among her closest friends in the Lords.

Lord John Peyton, who became another great friend to Lucy, describes the extraordinarily archaic ceremony of introduction:

> The newcomer and his [*sic*] sponsors wear robes, usually borrowed, and carry hats which you would never wear [...] outside the theatre. Without them the new entrant and his sponsors would not be able to salute the Lord Chancellor, who, so that he can respond, wears a three-

Lord Frederick Seebohm, Lucy Faithfull and Lady Young

Lucy Faithfull: mother to hundreds

cornered hat on top of his full-bottomed wig. Preceded by Garter King of Arms, who, parcelled up in the Royal Arms, looks rather like a King from a pack of cards, and followed by Black Rod, they march in, in line. When the new peer, on one knee, has presented his writ of summons to the Lord Chancellor and taken the oath, the three of them, guided by Garter, take their seats on one of the back-benches, put on their hats, rise, take them off again, and bow; having done so three times, they process out of the Chamber.[219]

It must have been galling for Barbara Kahan to see her long-standing rival elevated to the peerage like this. Kahan saw herself as someone who had got to where she was through sheer hard work, merit, determination and a thorough grasp of the issues, and here was this unintellectual Lucy, apparently floating rather more effortlessly up, being buddies with Baroness Young and those Oxford Tories, an establishment figure.

Lucy gave her maiden speech a month after her introduction, on 10 March, nailing her colours to the mast, speaking about the 'poverty trap'. She recommended a national minimum wage and raising the tax threshold to benefit small businesses and people on low incomes, a move away from means-tested benefits. She said,

> The poverty trap relates to low wage earners who, seeking to improve their quality of life are little or no better off if they achieve a small wage rise by working overtime or by taking a second job […] a man who is out of work can be better off than a man who is in work on a low wage. If a man's wage reaches a certain point he loses his entitlement to means-tested benefits, rent rebate, free school meals, and family income supplement. The tax threshold has fallen so low with rising inflation that even a low wage earner is now liable to income tax and, in certain circumstances, people drawing supplementary benefits[220] are also subject to tax. What one Department spends much time in giving,

another spends much time in taking away. She quoted
R.H. Tawney in 1913, "The continuance of social evils
is not due to the fact that we do not know what is right
but to the fact that we prefer to continue doing what is
wrong", a maxim that, in 2009, still rings horribly true.

She received a congratulatory note on her speech from John
Belstead, "The Conservative Party in the Lords is not perhaps as
strong as it might be on Social Science matters, and we are lucky
to have you here now", he wrote.

So Lucy joined the Lords the same month that Mrs Thatcher
took over leadership of the Conservative opposition from Edward
Heath. A year later, in March 1976, Harold Wilson resigned as
Prime Minister, to be replaced by James Callaghan, a very different
personality.

Why did she decide to become a Tory rather than a Labour
peer? This was the question in the minds of many social work
colleagues. (And not only on theirs, also on those of some fellow
Tories. Willie Whitelaw was once heard to enquire "Whose side
are you on, Lucy?") Conservative social policy, particularly in the
Thatcher years, was anathema to most social workers. Lucy had not
been a local Conservative Party member, and her political opinions
were largely unknown before she went into the Lords. A document
in her archive entitled "Loyalty in the House of Lords" gives one
answer. She wrote of herself:

> *Why am I a Conservative?* I believe that as far as possible
> and practicable each individual should be so equipped
> socially, educationally and health wise to be independent
> and self-reliant. But I believe that there should be a safety
> net of services both statutory and voluntary to support
> and care for the vulnerable; in the care of the young, the
> services given to them should as far as is possible, help
> them towards self-reliance and independence.

She elaborated on this in the Oxford University Sermon, which
she delivered in May 1995:

I do not believe in the total Welfare State, because it may tempt people to seek benefits without any effort to earn them and because it may encourage the notion of an Utopian society, in which everybody can enjoy everything that life has to offer. [...] What we are trying to do is to kindle whatever spark lies in each individual and light a flame of endeavour and aspiration.

So this was her brand of what would now be called caring Conservatism.

When Professor Jane Aldgate once asked her the same question, a slightly different, but equally believable, answer came back, "Well, I have thought about it, but you see, as a Tory peer, I have the ear of the Prime Minister at any point when I want it, and if I crossed the House, I wouldn't have that." She told Jane the story of the time when she and her allies were trying to persuade John Major (who became Prime Minister in 1990) of the necessity to change the legislation relating to young people leaving Care. At the time, children were discharged from Care in Children's Homes or foster

Lucy Faithfull seated in the Lords (woman second from left in third row).

parents between the ages of sixteen and eighteen, and were cast loose with often no-one to continue to take an interest in them or support them financially. It is hard to imagine how a teenager in the most secure and loving home could cope with having no support at all after eighteen; how much harder it was for young people who had been abused and/or neglected and whose families were perhaps forbidden from continuing to support them or were unable or unwilling to do so. There was no legal responsibility on Local Authorities after the child became eighteen. Lucy had arranged a meeting with John Major, who clearly had no grasp of the issues at all, and he'd said, "Well, I don't see what the problem is, Lucy. These children can return to their own families." She smiled, "The problem is, John, that these young people don't have families to go back to", whereupon, in her account, he'd replied, "Oh, goodness, I didn't know that"! That is why she stayed in the Tory party, because she felt she could be much more influential on that side of the House.[221]

A shrewd operator, Lucy always positioned herself in a particular place on the Lords benches in a strategic position in which she was well placed to catch the Speaker's eye. She also told her cousin Hugh Faithfull that she felt, by always sitting in the same place, people knew who and where she was. She got noticed in a way that people who sat in different places at different times did not. She also paid close attention to her clothes, favouring rich, bright colours, and pinning on a variety of eye-catching brooches, again, I suspect, so that she would stand out amongst the dark-suited men. That she was aware of the importance of fashion and self-presentation is shown by a letter to a fellow peeress:

> Many of us prefer Italian shoes because they are more comfortable and at the same time elegant. English shoes are so boring. [...] I went to a hen-party the other day; everyone of us was wearing a dress made abroad.[222]

Photos in her archive show her in a range of well-chosen outfits. For an Institute of Home Economics meeting at the House in April 1991 she wears a gorgeous claret velvet jacket with amber necklace and earrings.[223] Ruth Scarman, wife of Lord Leslie Scarman, was another friend with whom she discussed clothes. Ruth writes encouragingly to her, "A friend of mine is putting on a Dress Show in aid of Caldecott Homes [...] and there are some fairly large clothes for you and I to look at!"[224]

Winter heating allowance/needs of the elderly/homelessness

Lucy's contribution to debates in the Lords was invariably related to subjects she knew well from her social work career, and many of them were enlivened by anecdotes, perhaps slightly fictionalised, from her time in Social Services. In a debate in 1976 on winter heating allowances and the needs of the elderly, she argued for an adequate pension rate that included money for fuel, and for elderly people to be regarded "as people of independence, as people able to make a decision, and as people who are able to give to the community as well as receive". She goes on:

> I remember when I first became a director of social services being offered tickets for Wembley Ice Rink, and I rang up the matron of one of our old people's homes [...] and suggested that twenty of the old people should go to the ice rink. The matron said that they could not possibly go, that they would die. I replied, 'How can man die better than facing fearful odds?' They all put on their best hats, the men had their suits cleaned, and they went to the ice rink – and they did not die.[225]

She put in a word for the home helps, a group of workers who, I guess, are not much discussed in Westminster. They are, she said, mixing her metaphors somewhat, "the backbone and the salt of the earth". To cut their numbers would be a false economy, she maintained.

In the late 1970s, Lord Longford regularly initiated debates on the prison population; there was concern, as there still is now, about prison overcrowding. Lucy argued for a countrywide network of hostels. Foreshadowing her own difficulties with finding properties for the treatment of sex offenders, she told of the danger of hostels only being in some towns and not others, because then, "those of us who are trying to set up hostels have a double task, because we have to persuade the community to accept not only the people in their own area, but those from surrounding areas". She must have engaged the attention of the noble lords by the story she told to illustrate this:

> Walking along a street in Oxford, I saw the head of our Simon Community following a man who, quite clearly, was either a drug addict or had taken too much drink. He asked me whether I would watch the man while he fetched his car, so the man and I sat together on the pavement, and by way of conversation I asked him where he had come from. He said that he had come from a Midlands town, so I asked him what he was doing in Oxford. He replied that his town had no hostel and he was told he had better make his way to Oxford because there he would find a Simon Community'.[226]

She acknowledged the attraction of warmth and regular food in prison for this type of homeless man, frequently retelling the story of her friend Jim – later becoming Joe at one point – who used to call on her a week before Christmas to wish her the compliments of the season. When she protested that he was a bit early, he used to reply he had 'business' to do before Christmas, meaning to clock a policeman, knock him out, appear before the magistrates and be sentenced to a short time in prison, where he would be given a Christmas dinner.[227]

She went on to address the underlying reasons for people being in prison, their deprived or difficult childhoods, and emphasised the importance of policies to support families if the prison population were to be reduced. "Wordsworth was perhaps right when he said: 'The child is father to the man', she said, and we have still not learned this lesson. Prisons now are more overcrowded than they were in Lucy's day.

Education Bill 1976 – Social Work education

A great deal of Parliamentary time in that autumn of 1976 was taken up with debates on the Education Bill. It dealt mainly with the setting up of comprehensive schools, of which Lucy was not a supporter, but she took the opportunity to explain to their Lordships the intricacies of education for the social work profession, asking that grants for social work students be made mandatory, rather than discretionary. She had done her research.

> This qualification [the Certificate of Qualification in Social Work] is achieved after full-time two-year training. There are 127 courses, 58 in universities and [...] 69 in polytechnics and other colleges. [...] In this county we have 13 per cent untrained probation and after-care officers, and 60 per cent untrained field social workers [...] The present position is that there are no [fewer] than four methods by which social work students may be funded [...] first, probation and after-care trainees are seconded from probation departments and funded by the Home Office. Second, graduates applying to do the course are funded from the Department of Health and Social Security. Third, social service departments take on trainee social workers. After some time, and if such trainees are suitable, they are seconded for training on a salary to a course. Fourth?

She continued the theme in a major debate on Social Workers the following Spring, pointing out that, as a result of cutbacks in Local Authority budgets, Councils were having to choose between cutting services to those in need or cutting Social Work training secondments. She anticipated a crisis the following autumn when 36% of places on social work courses were likely to be unfilled because of lack of funding, in the context of an already woefully low level of qualification across the profession. Fast forward to 1983 and she was at it again, this time in the context of the development of care in the community:

If there are complaints from magistrates or judges that social workers do not know their law or court procedures then there is an outcry from the public through the media and from other professionals [...] Yet the authorities are not prepared to train social workers under the mandatory system. Social workers cannot have laid at their door that they are not doing their job properly if society – the taxpayer – is not prepared to pay.[228]

Fast forward again, this time as far as 1995, and she was initiating a Lords' debate on social workers' training, citing the pressure on social workers from ever-increasing legislation they have to implement, and from the "explosion of awareness and concern of child sexual abuse, little acknowledged in years gone by". She asked pointedly, "I wonder whether the heavy responsibilities placed by statute on social workers are generally appreciated. They have to make decisions that affect the liberty of citizens." She pointed out that:

Doctors have a five-year or longer training; health visitors have a four-year training; teachers have a three-year training; the social worker is often the person to call a case conference and in some cases to play the leading role, yet he or she is the least qualified among his or her professional colleagues. [Furthermore] Social workers in the European Union have a longer training than those in the UK.[229]

She recommended that training at University degree level would be the way to reinforce the skills and knowledge of social workers, but despite all her efforts throughout her years in the Lords, it was not until 2003 that Social Work became an exclusively degree-level qualification. It is a national scandal that it is only in the aftermath of the Baby Peter tragedy that Lord Laming is able to appeal in 2009 for major government investment in social worker training.

Lucy Faithfull: mother to hundreds

Under fives

A theme of Lucy's in the Lords was her campaign for a coherent policy from the government for the under fives. She was articulate in emphasising the importance of the first few years of life and fundamental parental attachment for the emotional health of the child, quoting her friend Winnicott, as well as research from the National Children's Bureau and the Tavistock Clinic to back up her arguments, and bringing in stories from her own experience of deprived and neglected children in Oxford. Expenditure on this young age group, she argued, prevented much greater public expenditure in the future on older children who had never established parental attachments and who needed care or became delinquent. In a debate in 1980, she lists her qualifications to talk on this subject, mentioning that she had worked in a nursery school, and listing the voluntary organisations she was linked with, for example the National Association of Nursery Matrons (of which she was president) and the Pre-school Playgroups Association. Nevertheless (as in her evacuation days), Lucy was against universal provision of nursery education on the grounds that young children are best cared for by their mothers, supported by access to playgroups.

The broadcaster Libby Purves put Lucy on the spot during a Radio 4 interview on *Midweek*.[230] She pointed out that Lucy had had a successful career, and, like most professional women of her generation, did not have children. She went on to ask whether Lucy thought women had the right to have both children and a career. Lucy answered that they do, but should not go out to work when their children are young. "Outstanding women can start at thirty-five and get to the top. If a woman has the capacity, she can get to the top," she asserted.

Conferences

Alongside her work in the Lords, Lucy was an enthusiastic conference attender, and keynote speech-giver. Going to conferences was one way in which she kept herself in touch with current issues in the social work field. She also had great fun. At the Social Care Association conference at the Imperial Hotel, Blackpool in 1977, Dick Clough, that year's President, who was a single man, invited her to act as his 'consort'. The town's Mayor, who had enjoyed himself enormously at the closing dinner, got into hilarious cross purposes when he overheard Lucy talking about 'peers', and interjected "We've got one of those!" (meaning Blackpool pier). Towards the end of the evening, Dick and Lucy finally managed to get him away from the bar and safely into his official car with his wife and his chaplain. They returned to the ballroom collapsing with laughter, and prepared to dance together, only to find that a role-play game was in progress. Dick had to be St George, pretending to slay Lucy as the dragon who was crawling around the ballroom floor on hands and knees in a gorgeous pink ball gown.

Summer frocks as well as evening dresses were needed for her next trip, to Malawi, in October 1977, as part of a parliamentary delegation of three women at the invitation of Dr Hastings Banda. In photos, she looks at ease with her African hosts, attending a round of formal visits and receptions.

Much warmer clothes were needed for her next excursion, a walking holiday with friends in the Lake District, staying at the Wateredge Hotel in Ambleside, and photos show her at Tarn Hows and snow-covered Langdale Pike, wrapped against the cold in a large cagoule, woolly hat and heavy boots.

In February 1978, Lord Leslie Scarman was installed as Chancellor of the University of Warwick.[231] The new Chancellor could choose a list of people to receive honorary degrees, and he chose Lucy for a D.Litt. She was overjoyed. In her formal acceptance letter to the Vice Chancellor (who was John Butterworth, husband of her friend in the House of Lords, Lady Doris Butterworth), she wrote that she would like to think that the honour would be regarded as "adding lustre" to her fellow social workers and Directors of Social Services. She also enthusiastically told Lord Scarman:

I am not an academic. As a social worker, my experience, the lessons I have learned, and, one could say, the books I have read, consisted of the intimate lives of people, particularly those in trouble and in need.

Lucy became great friends with Lord Scarman and his wife Ruth, and went to stay with them in their house in Kent and invited them back to Oxford. Ruth refers in one letter to 'Leigh's blonde', the only reference I have found to Leigh's private life away from Lucy.

Protection of Children Bill 1978

The Protection of Children Bill had started life as a private members' bill in the Commons early in 1978, but Lucy introduced it in the Lords for Second Reading and Committee stages. It raised the previously ignored and highly controversial issue of pornographic photography of children. (It was only a few years earlier that Lord Longford had published his report clarifying the pernicious nature of pornography, which had earned him the title 'Lord Porn' in the London press.) Lucy pointed out that this pornographic photography of children was a form of abuse – the lens is pointed at a real child. This must have been an unpopular Bill to champion. Who wants to think about such distasteful and distressing things, especially in the elegant Pugin chambers of Westminster? She had to contend with peers denying that the problem existed. Prominent among these was Lord Houghton of Sowerby. He maintained that, by discussing this issue, Parliament had been subjected to "a campaign of hysteria, emotion and pressure unexampled in my experience of nearly thirty years in Parliament." An Act outlawing this kind of photography had been passed in the United States Congress earlier in the year. Lord Houghton went to the US looking for, and failing to find, "that load of pornography that, we were told, would swamp this country if we did not have this Bill to stop it." Lucy, perhaps with some sarcasm, asked him whether he had asked "any Congressmen or members of the Senate [...] why they passed a Bill in February of this year as an Amendment of the Child Protection Bill [and] Secondly did the noble Lord contact the Odyssey Institute in New York which produced the figures and the statistics upon which the Bill, subsequently the Act in the United States, was passed?"[232] He, unlike she, had not done his homework thoroughly, and had no answer. When passed, the Act made it an offence to take, permit to be taken, make, possess, show, distribute or advertise indecent images of children.[233]

At the general election of 1979, following the "Winter of Discontent", the Tories, under Margaret Thatcher, defeated Labour. Lucy's friend, Janet Young, was made minister for Education and Science, outside the cabinet, and, in September 1981, she became the first woman to hold the post of leader of the House of Lords. An influential friend for Lucy to have.

Charity Commission

Lucy's presence on the Lords' benches must have enlivened what were often turgid debates. The BBC TV programme *The Week in the Lords,* broadcast during the 1980s, often showed elderly peers nodding and snoozing behind whichever speaker was holding forth. Lucy was never one of these. In January 1987, the Lords were debating the dire state of the Charity Commission, alleging that it was understaffed and overloaded with work, and allowing lax practices, for example, not following up charities that failed to submit their annual accounts. (Foreshadowing the shortcomings of Gracewell.) Lucy was arguing that malpractice did indeed go on. At the time, she had her arm in plaster after a fall. She declared, "If every noble lord were to sign my plaster, and I sell it for charity, and keep 80% of the money and only give 20% to charity, no-one would question me!" This must have made the more somnolent of her colleagues sit up and take notice.

Mental Health Bill – ASWs

Lucy's frontline social work gave her great credibility during debates in 1981 on the Mental Health Bill (amending the 1959

Mental Health Act). Despite worries about funding, she supported the introduction of specialist training for Approved Social Workers (ASWs), arguing that the basic generic social work training was inadequate (as indeed it was). The intensity of her background lobbying is illustrated by a comment from Lord Elton, then a minister at the DHSS. He commented during the debate, "It is always dangerous to encourage the noble baroness to write to one at length, because she is apt to do so without encouragement!" She argued for the ASW, rather than the nearest relative, to have the power to make the decision to section a patient to psychiatric hospital. The relative would not necessarily know the alternatives to hospital that there may be in the local area. Also there are implications for the future of the relationship between patient and relative if the latter is the person who commits the former to hospital compulsorily. She points to the importance of personal relationships between both social workers and doctors, but more importantly between the social worker and her client,

> I must tell your lordships that I was called out at about three in the morning to section a boy who absolutely refused to go into mental hospital [...] I had known that boy for ten years. The only reason why he would not go into hospital was that he wanted to know who was going to look after his dog, which was called Buster. Because I knew that it was the only thing in the world he loved, I said to him, 'I will look after Buster' – which was a great sacrifice, I might say – 'if you will go into mental hospital.' He did.[234]

The 1985 Social Security Act

Back in 1980, Lucy had been arguing against the abolition of the Supplementary Benefits Commission, reflecting the anxieties of social workers that issues of financial support would fall increasingly onto their shoulders. She said that social workers and probation officers are already in a position whereby they cannot fulfil their statutory duties because they are so busy negotiating with Social Security on behalf of clients. She pressed for more mature Social Security counter staff and more pleasant offices.

The Social Security Act 1985 was the cause of my leaving frontline social work. It replaced the system of Supplementary Benefits that had been set up in 1976 with the Social Fund and 'Income Support'. Lucy gives their Lordships examples of urgent need such as terminally ill people, or women who are 'cruelly treated' and go to Women's Aid who, under the previous system, would receive a one-off grant.[235] The Social Fund would provide only a crisis loan, which would be 'discretionary' and subject to a finite annual budget, and would need to be paid back. The idea that people in poverty and on state benefits could somehow budget their already minuscule income so that they could repay money they needed urgently seemed to me, and to Lucy, to be harsh and unrealistic. She argued consistently in favour of grants rather than loans.

The Education Reform Act 1988

The main initiatives of this Bill were to introduce local management of schools and to set up Ofsted. Lucy, however, was concerned about the provision for children with special needs. The Voluntary Council for Handicapped Children wrote to thank Lucy for her commitment, tireless energy, enthusiasm, and "of course political acumen and diplomacy" in ensuring that the Act should promote educational opportunities for children with disabilities and special needs. "We are very conscious of the great burden of work which we placed upon your shoulders over the last few months." It is, they say, "a massive and complex piece of legislation."[236] Lucy's ability to orchestrate a strong cross-Party group within the House of Lords was crucial.

Family Court

It may have been her Scottish blood, and the fact that she spent holidays in Scotland that first aroused Lucy's interest in the juvenile justice system North of the border. The Social Work (Scotland) Act of 1968 had replaced the juvenile court system by a system of Children's Hearings,[237] following the recommendations by the famous report by Lord Kilbrandon. Lucy felt that the present juvenile court system in England and Wales intimidated children and parents, who often did not understand what was happening, or what had been decided. Many lawyers felt that the adversarial nature of the proceedings encouraged polarised views and worsening of conflict. Family jurisdiction took place at several levels: in the high court, the county courts and in the civil side of juvenile courts. Lucy thought that a family court should absorb these functions. The debate at the time was between those who favoured a family court which encompassed a criminal jurisdiction and those who wanted to confine a family court to family matters and who argued for the retention of a juvenile court model to deal with juvenile crime. In addition to belonging to the Family Courts Campaign, founded in 1984, Lucy had become the Chairman of a group called "New Approaches to Juvenile Crime" whose members were drawn from eight organisations working with young offenders.[238] The campaign certainly kept her busy. She told Don Brand:

> I am speaking up and down the country. I have been
> to Coventry, Norwich, Northumberland, and am going
> to Sheffield and Bradford. I am seeing Leon Brittan at
> the Home Office on Thursday and Patrick Jenkin next
> week.[239]

In 1983 the New Approaches group commissioned a study of the comparative structures of the juvenile justice system in England and Wales, *Juvenile Justice in the United Kingdom*, which illustrated the case for a change. In November 1987, Lucy moved an amendment to the Criminal Justice Bill advocating the introduction into England and Wales of a children's hearing system similar to the system in Scotland. Despite her persuasive arguments, she was not successful in carrying this idea forward. The Lord Chancellor, Lord Mackay's view was that a Family Court system would be too expensive to implement.[240] The debate was to continue as part of the discussions around the Children Bill.

Children Bill

Lucy's greatest achievement in the House of Lords, and the one for which she is always remembered by everyone in the field of child care, is in her role as part of a 'double act'[241] with Lord Mackay, the Lord Chancellor, in steering the Children Bill through the House of Lords. This became the Children Act 1989, one of the most significant pieces of legislation affecting children of the twentieth century. The principle of the Act was to create a uniform and coherent framework for the different strands of child care law that had developed largely separately over the past few hundred years. These related to children in public care, children caught up in private legal battles, for example in custody and access in divorce, children in Wardship, and children subject to abuse. An important impetus for change in the mid 1980s came from a number of reports into child death scandals, and the alleged failures of the existing systems to protect children. The most important of these were the inquiry into the death of Jasmine Beckford in 1985[242] and the controversy surrounding the handling of the alleged child sexual abuse in Cleveland in 1988.

Over a period of years Lucy worked on the Bill in the All-Party Parliamentary Group for Children,[243] which she had established and chaired from 1981 until her death, and she helped to draft discussion documents and amendments, and the Bill itself. The Annual Review of the APPGC for1988-89 rightly says:

> Baroness Faithfull played an important role in bringing together expert opinion of the Bill from voluntary, statutory and professional organisations to advise parliamentarians from all parties in both Houses of Parliament. As a result, a considerable measure of agreement was reached on key amendments and the Group was able to assist in improving the Bill at all stages of its progress.

Lucy Faithfull: mother to hundreds

Most of Lucy's characteristic contributions to the debates on the long series of amendments to the Bill were rooted in her Social Services experience. She argued against children being received into Care as a result of homelessness, upbraiding the Lord Chancellor for his naïveté in thinking this didn't happen – "I am afraid that the noble and learned lord is far more trusting than I am. I know the homeless legislation very well; it has not always been administered as we would wish it".[244]

Reading the accounts of the debates on the Bill in *Hansard* one sometimes suspects that Lucy was not above using the occasional story that was not quite accurate if it made a point more vivid, and served her cause. "She was very shrewd, was our Lucy. She'd never set out to deceive, but she would certainly want to put the best possible light on the argument", says Tom White. She talks of crossing Magdalen Bridge and coming across a young man who had been in Oxford City's Care. She apparently gave him a guitar, which helped him become one of the most successful pop musicians in France and completely changed his life. Was this all her doing, one wonders?

The points she put during the debates were well argued, and many of them were incorporated in the final Act. Among these were that children should be present at their statutory reviews, that siblings should be placed wherever possible in foster care together, that relatives acting as foster parents should receive payments, that the phrase foster 'parents' should be changed to foster 'carers', that parents with children in voluntary care should have to give notice of their intention to remove the child, and that Guardians ad Litem (who represent the child's voice in court) should be better supported and organised. She argued that generic social workers needed specialist child care training, although she wanted this to be as part of the initial course, rather than as a post-Qualifying award.

> If, as is recommended in the Cleveland Report,[245] there is to be closer collaboration between those working in the area of child protection then the social workers must be skilled in their own spheres in order to work with

colleagues from the other relevant professions, particularly as the social worker is often the key worker in child protection cases and the one who is usually responsible for taking a case to court.[246]

She argued fiercely, against weighty opposition, to prohibit foster carers from inflicting corporal punishment. The Lord Chancellor said that as foster parents are expected to bring up children as members of their own family it is illogical that they can beat their own children and not the foster children. Lord Mottistone told the House that such punishment never did him any harm. Lucy leaped to her feet.

> Lord Mottistone has had a wonderful life and could tolerate having a good old whang and battering. Children in foster homes are vulnerable and often have deep emotional feelings of animosity against life. One does not want to add to that.[247]

The area of debate where Lucy's contribution was particularly strong was that of the support for children leaving Care. The main spokesperson on the Children Bill from the Labour Party was Lucy's friend Lady Nora David, and, despite Nora's position on the opposite benches, they supported each other in debates.[248] They both strongly argued that it is necessary for Local Authorities to continue to support young people until they are at least 21. Children in normal households, Lucy pointed out, continue to be helped by their families, often live at home and are considered part of the family in every respect, whereas young people in Care are thrown out of their foster homes or children's homes when they reach 18, usually utterly unprepared for such independence. There were long and ultimately fruitless debates on whether financial support for care leavers should come from the Social Security system, Lucy arguing that it should, as a statutory right.

On one occasion, Jane Tunstill, then at the National Council for Voluntary Child Care Organisations (NCVCCO), got together a group of young people from all over the country to go to the

House of Lords to talk to peers and MPs about why a section of the Bill on care leavers needed amending. Amongst them was one particularly angry girl with spiky hair and multiple body piercings, an articulate and aggressive talker. Lucy chaired the meeting and was "absolutely brilliant," Jane says. She was completely unfazed, listening attentively and speaking to the group as equals. Their lordships were very impressed. In subsequent debates, many who had met these young people made powerful speeches in favour of support for care leavers. Lord Prys-Davies was one of these. He said:

> Those members of your Lordships' House who last
> week in Committee Room 3 met thirty or forty young
> people who had left care were immensely moved by the
> experience which they related to us. I for one see their
> problems, their disadvantages and their travails in a much
> clearer way. I now understand why they are described as
> probably the most vulnerable section of that vulnerable
> age group.[249]

Baroness David publicly thanked Lucy for arranging the meeting, saying:

> It was a great feat of organisation. They were shown
> around the House, they were brought into the Chamber
> [...] We admire the noble Baroness very much for having
> done that and it was a great help to us.[250]

NHS and Community Care Act

Alongside the Children Act 1989, the other main legislation affecting the work of Social Services at that time was the NHS and Community Care Act 1990. Lucy and the APPGC were concerned about the possible fragmentation of children's health services, which could arise from the promotion of an internal market within the NHS. Although not relating to her main concern, children, Lucy took an energetic part in the debates as the Bill went through the Lords, drawing, as ever, on her own experiences as Social Services Director. For example, arguing for professionals to have right of entry to the property of people who are resistant in accepting the help they need, she told their Lordships:

> I arrived home one evening and opened the evening
> paper to see an article entitled, 'Director of Social Services
> Allows Old Lady to Die'. I immediately looked into
> the matter. I found that the old lady had not been out
> for weeks, she would not allow anybody into the house.
> Gradually she became weaker and weaker. Health visitors,
> doctors and social workers were not admitted, and
> ultimately she died.

She piled on the agony involved in dealing with the 'hard to help':

> A doctor telephoned me about an old man suffering from
> hypothermia. We sent in a social worker who lit the gas
> fire, took him hot soup and stayed with him for an hour
> or two. She went away and returned two hours later. The
> moment she [had gone] out of the door, he [had] hopped
> out of bed, switched off the gas fire and [he] refused to
> drink the soup.[251]

She was a supporter of the proposal of giving direct payments from Social Services budgets to allow people with a disability the flexibility to purchase their own care, giving the House an example of the people for whom the scheme would be appropriate:

> A fortnight ago I went to a conference at the Kings' Fund
> Centre and sat between two severely handicapped people.
> Neither of them had legs, but they lived in a flat on their
> own. The woman was a writer and the man was in the
> publishing business. They were perfectly capable of looking
> after themselves mentally and of ordering their own lives.

As the only social worker in the House, Lucy's 'human interest' stories must have enabled her colleagues on the benches to put flesh on the bones of their task of legislation drafting and amending.

APPGC

Apart from its role in the work on the Children Bill, the All–Party Parliamentary Group for Children took up a lot of Lucy's time and effort in the Lords from 1981 until her death. This group was created using funds from the International Year of the Child. Lucy, together with Jock Stollard MP, had been on the IYC Panel. The inaugural meeting took place in the Moses Room at Westminster in March 1981. The group was initially serviced by the NCVCCO. From the start, Lucy ensured that the Group's meetings would be lively and attract interested members of both Houses. On 24th June 1981, the subject was Intermediate Treatment (*see Chapter 4*). A group of young people who had been in trouble in Nottingham gave first-hand accounts of their experiences. "This enabled members to talk about the problems of juvenile delinquency with young people who would be directly affected by the forthcoming legislation changes," say the notes of the meeting. For a period, the Group produced a bi-weekly mailing, "Children and Parliament", of extracts from *Hansard* relevant to children's issues.

The IYC funding ended in 1983 and from the following year the National Children's Bureau (NCB) took over as the secretariat for the Group, with salaried staff, and Lucy energetically fundraised for this. She worked closely with Dr Ron Davie, NCB's second director. (The first had been Mia Kellmer-Pringle.)

Lucy had further links with the National Children's Bureau[252] from 1985 when she was elected President, succeeding Lord Wolfendon. Joan Cooper had been instrumental in setting up the Bureau, and was Vice-President. At the very same meeting, Barbara Kahan, Lucy's Oxfordshire rival, was made Chairman. This must have been a tricky situation, as Barbara made no secret of the fact that she felt Lucy was lightweight. Ron Davie writes:

> I was immensely pleased at Lucy's becoming President
> because I was moving the Bureau from its position when
> I took over [...] as 'a research and publishing house'
> to one where it was becoming ever more centred on

development and policy. Having a President who was a key figure in the Lords on children's affairs was an outward and visible sign of this, but also kept the Bureau close to the political (not party political, of course) action, since she had fairly ready access to Ministers and, indeed, to the P.M.[253]

In 1990, after a period of staff unhappiness, Ron Davie had been dismissed by Barbara. His view was that she came to the Bureau with a reputation of a person who felt the need to control what she touched, and says that "the term 'supportive' is not one which springs readily to mind!"[254] According to Simon Rodway, Lucy supported Davie and would not have wanted him to go. Lucy went with Simon to Ron Davie's leaving party. Lucy was due to spend the night with Simon at his house in Chiswick. At around midnight, he suggested to Lucy that it was time to leave. "Oh, we can't go yet, the night is young", she replied, and remained the life and soul of the party until the early hours. When John Rea Price joined the Bureau in 1990, "a tornado had swept through the place", he

Lucy Faithfull with Diana, Princess of Wales, in 1989.

Lucy Faithfull: mother to hundreds

says, and it was "falling apart".[255] Barbara Kahan did a good job, he thinks, in holding the Bureau together.

In her capacity as President it fell to Lucy to welcome Diana, Princess of Wales, on the occasion of her visit to the Bureau to celebrate its 25th anniversary in 1989.[256]

Virginia Bottomley was in the Commons while Lucy was in the Lords. She had known Lucy from a young age, as she comes from an old Oxford family, the Garnetts. She also knew Lucy as Chair of the All-Party Parliamentary Group for Children. (Bottomley was soon made a minister and became too much taken up with government issues to attend the Group for very long.) She points out that there were relatively few people in Parliament as a whole who took Lucy's social science approach to issues. It was an approach pioneered by that very different personality, Barbara Wootton, before her.[257] She says of Lucy that she had the integrity, compassion and charisma that are necessary in Parliament. She adds, "She had personal authority, and great charm. She could be both hectoring and flirtatious at the same time. She came straight to the point, and these techniques were very effective even with very senior ministers."[258] In 1994, Lucy wrote to Bottomley, then Secretary of State for Health, recommending John Chant, Director of Social Work at Lothian Regional Council, for a peerage. "There are several doctors in the House; there are several educationalists, industrialists, bankers, etc. and one benighted social worker, that is me! I would welcome a colleague," she appeals, but without result.

Daphne Park

A great friend of Lucy's in the Lords was Daphne Park. They had met while Daphne was Principal of Somerville College, Oxford in the early eighties. She and Lucy used to go to dinner with each other in Oxford. Lucy was usually accompanied by her brother Leigh, who, by that stage, was deaf, so unable to take much part in the conversation. He did not live with Lucy, but was often staying with her in Woodstock Road. One evening at dinner, Lucy announced she had booked for the three of them to go on a Swan

Hellenic cruise. She told Daphne:"If you don't want to come you've got twenty-four hours to decide before the money has to be paid." Daphne decided to go, and they had a wonderful time sailing around the Greek islands, lubricated by six Whisky Macs a day, two before lunch and more before dinner. This was 1982 or '83. They went on two subsequent cruises, and a third one after Leigh had died, "but the Greek one was the best", says Daphne.

After Lucy had divided her Woodstock Road house into two flats she occupied the first floor and let out the ground floor to visiting academic families. At one time Lucy had suggested to Daphne that she might like to live in this downstairs flat. Daphne refused, because she knew that if one of them were going out she would feel obliged to see if the other would like to come; they would each be aware if the other were alone and feel they should invite her for tea, and so on. It would damage their friendship, she felt.[259] One of the tenants who did live downstairs provided Lucy with a tribute in the form of another limerick. It is entitled 'Observations from Below', but the scansion leaves something to be desired:

> In Oxford there lives a lady quite delightful,
> Whose working hours are simply frightful:
> How do you suppose
> With so little repose,
> She remains so pleasant and so insightful.[260]

Daphne Park had a distinguished career as one of MI6's senior controllers, running agents in Moscow during the Cold War, and infiltrating Hanoi during the Vietnam War. To celebrate Daphne's retirement in 1990, Lucy drove her to the bookshop and literary festival town of Hay-on-Wye in her little car, which Daphne stuffed full of the books she'd bought as her retirement present to herself. I guess Lucy and Daphne's friendship must have been based on the great deal they had in common. Both had an African childhood, both were separated from their parents at an early age, both lived in Oxford, both remained unmarried and both were made Tory peers on their retirement from their respective careers.

Daphne lived in Observatory Street, off the Woodstock Road, and Lucy used to go round to her flat for some peace and quiet to work, because at her own flat she was always bombarded with phone-calls and visitors, many of them ex-clients. People knew where she lived and she was the one person they wanted to talk to if they were in difficulties. She would bring her parliamentary papers to Daphne's; they would have a snack lunch and work away in separate rooms.

When Daphne entered the House of Lords Lucy acted as her sponsor, which Daphne thinks was hugely to her advantage. She gained credibility as a protégée of Lucy's. Lucy was also a mentor to her, advising her not to make a speech for at least two or three months, until she'd completely understood the protocol. Lucy and Daphne would drive down from Oxford to Westminster together. They would use the journey to talk, not about personal things, but more of difficult encounters they'd had, of issues of the minute, and to let off steam with one another. Daphne, like Lucy, had reservations about various aspects of Tory policy. Lucy passed on to her the benefit of her own philosophy, and advised her to vote against her own party only on issues on which she felt particularly strongly and was expert, otherwise vote with them.

Leigh's death

Leigh had fallen ill. Like Lucy, he had developed colon cancer. Because their father had died so young, it is difficult to determine whether there had been a genetic disposition to this cancer through the family, for both siblings to be afflicted with it. Lucy's friend, the surgeon Malcolm Gough, thinks that, unlike Lucy, Leigh ignored the early symptoms, until it was too late. Leigh was operated on, but the prognosis was poor. He went to convalesce on the Isle of Wight. It was Daphne Park's driver who went to fetch him, but, on the way back, Leigh had a sort of seizure. The driver only just managed to get him to the Acland hospital, where, in February 1990, he died. Lucy was beside him, and it was she who registered his death. She scattered his ashes behind her garden at

Woodstock Road in the grounds of St Edward's School. She had been very fond of Leigh; he was very important to her, and she was very upset at his death. She had lost her only remaining close relative and also her travelling companion. She had made plans to go with him to India, China, and Japan. She sadly told Drew Clode: "Well, I shan't do the travelling now because my brother has died. One doesn't do these things on one's own". It was at this sad time that she made an inventory of things in his cottage in East Meon.

Malcolm and Sheila Gough did their best to support Lucy in her bereavement, inviting her on holiday with them to Tuscany in April, and taking her to Glyndebourne. They say she became almost part of their family. Lucy often returned their hospitality by inviting them to Christmas carol concerts at Christchurch, for which tickets are at a premium. These concerts were followed by stylish tea parties in the college. The threesome also went to the theatre at Stratford-on-Avon, notably on one foggy night in January 1993.

Lucy took a short, and perhaps enforced, break from the House of Lords, while she grieved and worked to settle her brother's affairs, returning to action at the beginning of May. She had a punishing schedule for an 80-year-old. In August, she was in America, staying with her several cousins,[261] as she did every summer, at their house in the country near Bedford, Massachusetts. Then, in September, her plans, as outlined to Peter Smith, were:

> 10th–13th – Cumberland Lodge,
> 14th – Caldecott Community meeting
> Monday 17th – Free, in Oxford
> 18th–20th – Association of Directors of Social Services
>   Conference
> 21st – Free
> Monday 24th – Meeting on Family Courts[262]

This was a fairly typical fortnight.

That, despite this punishing schedule, she did look after her health as much as she could is shown by a letter she wrote to her temporary secretary, Margaret, saying:[263]

> I had my blood pressure taken at Inglewood – the nurse said, 'You have the heart of a young girl'. That was most encouraging at 82!!! [...] I managed to lose 3 ½ lbs at the Health Hydro so I am now 10 stone 6 lbs, which is still too much. I must get down to 9 stone 12 lbs.

Perch in London

I had expected to find that Lucy had rented some sort of pied-à-terre in London so that she could attend the Lords without having to drive back to Oxford late at night. But I found instead that what she called her "perch" in London was with her long-standing friend Nanette Borrie, whom she had met when they both had a flat in Harrington Gardens, South Kensington in the 1950s (while Lucy was working at the Home Office). There they used to go to each other's parties, and Nanette stayed with Lucy in Oxford, where she met Leigh. After her cancer operation, Lucy had been to recuperate with Nanette and her husband, who by that time had a cottage in Devon. By the 1970s, they were living in a newly built house near Wimbledon Common, at 1 Alfreton Close, Parkside, and they offered her a room on a permanent basis. Lucy was not the person to jump on the 'second home' expenses gravy train. Lucy called the Borrie's house "home", as in "I'll be home at [...]" When she came in late at night, Nanette would make her a drink and she would gossip about things that had happened at the House of Lords that day.

Nanette remembers a night with Lucy at the tiny Orange Tree theatre in Richmond. "When the play ended we stood up to go out, and jolly music was playing. Lucy took off and started dancing, and before long she was joined by some of the audience". Nanette had family in Australia and often went out there for extended periods, handing lodger Lucy over for safekeeping to her neighbours, Stuart and Jilly Holden. They also found her delightful, if untidy, company; she always had huge piles of books beside her bed. They visited her in Woodstock Road, and comment that, although her flat was always very untidy, Lucy knew exactly where everything was. She kept her walking boots in the back of her Vauxhall Astra, and used to put them on to tramp across Wimbledon Common or out in Kent when she was visiting Caldecott. Lucy and Jilly talked clothes. Jilly admired the brooches she always wore on her lapel. Lucy would say, "How do I look? I must look smart today; I have this meeting to chair." Lucy had a necklace of beautiful citrine stones that she had inherited from her mother Bessie, which was too long, and Jilly had a ring made from one of the stones. She was so glad she did, because Lucy later lost the necklace when it was in a suitcase that was stolen from her car, which upset her greatly. When the Holden's adolescent son was having difficulties, Lucy gave helpful advice, and she was also very supportive of their daughter Minnie when she went up to Oxford in 1989. Minnie now keeps a photo of Lucy in her dining room.

Eightieth birthday and Hon. Fellowship

For Lucy's eightieth birthday in December 1990, her friends Malcolm Gough, her surgeon, and his wife Sheila, gave a private party for her at their house. A more formal dinner was held in the Cholmondley Room in the House of Lords (with its terrace overlooking the Thames). Terry Philpot remembers that Lucy's old friend, Lord Seebohm, hosted it, and that the guests included none other than Barbara Kahan as well as such other social work luminaries as Joan Cooper.

Lucy's Oxford connections, meanwhile, had not been forgotten. In March 1992, St Hilda's College offered her an Honorary Fellowship. The proposal for her election informs the governing body of the College that, "Baroness Faithfull is currently a very active member in the House. She is known for her personal integrity in political and all other issues". She accepted with alacrity. This honour thrilled her, as had the Hon. MA in 1973, conscious as she was of her lack of a first degree. Dame Elizabeth

Butler-Sloss writes to her from the Royal Courts of Justice: "I am delighted to learn that St Hilda's has had the wisdom to ask you to join us". [264]

She entered the last six years of her life with plenty of issues still to occupy her, foremost among these being juvenile justice, an issue on which she battled long and hard against her Tory party in the form of Michael Howard, the then Home Secretary, in particular.

Notes:

[210] Matthew Hart, *The Irish Game: A True Story of Crime and Art* (NY: Walkerbooks, 2002).

[211] This story was related to me by Terry Philpot who had heard it from Lucy herself.

[212] Letter, LF to Don Brand, 25 January 1976.

[213] Indeed no woman had been admitted to the House of Lords until 1958, and then only with stiff opposition from some male peers.

[214] This story was told by Lady Daphne Park in her address at Lucy's funeral.

[215] Tom White admitted candidly that the other possible candidates for a peerage were all men, and indeed the ADSS (Association of Directors of Social Services), unlike the ACO, was a male-dominated organisation. There was no female President until Mary Sugden held that office in 1981.

[216] Letter LF to Henry Maddock, 9 January 1976.

[217] Letter, LF to J.W. Freeman, (Director of Social Services at Leeds City Council) 26 January 1976.

[218] Bea Serota had been a member of the Seebohm Committee.

[219] John Peyton, *Without Benefit of Laundry: the autobiography of John Peyton*, (London: Bloomsbury, 1997).

[220] The Supplementary Benefits system was replaced by Income Support and the Social Fund in 1988, a move that Lucy staunchly opposed on the grounds that I.S. does not adequately support those in urgent need. She consistently argued in favour of grants rather than loans. [See HL Deb. 10 March 1976 Vol. 368 c. 1317.]

[221] Jane Aldgate, personal communication.

[222] Letter, LF to Baroness Jean Denton, 9 January 1993

[223] In the photo Lucy is being presented with a book by the Institute.

[224] Letter, Ruth Scarman to LF, 15 July 1987.

[225] HL Deb. 23 June 1976 Vol. 372 c. 351.

226 HL Deb. 5 July 1976 Vol. 372 c. 1111.

227 Ibid, c. 1112.

228 HL Deb. 9 December 1982 Vol. 437 c. 313.

229 HL Deb. 19 April 1995 Vol. 563 c. 517.

230 *Midweek*, 15 December 1993.

231 This nomination could be connected with the fact that Lord Scarman had recently chaired the enquiry into the Red Lion Square disorders in which Warwick University student Kevin Gately died. He went on to produce the reports on the controversial Grunwick dispute (1977) and the Brixton riots (1981).

232 HL Deb. 20 June 1978 Vol. 393 c. 1063.

233 Under the 1978 Act mere possession of indecent photographs of children was not outlawed. This was remedied by Section 160 of the Criminal Justice Act of 1988, which made possession an arrestable offence carrying a maximum sentence of 5 years' imprisonment. (Making an image, including downloading from the internet, now carries a maximum sentence of 10 years' imprisonment.)

234 HL Deb. 1 December 1981 Vol. 425 c. 1166.

235 HL Deb. 23 July 1986 Vol. 477 c. 52.

236 Letter, Philippa Russell, Principal Officer, to LF, 9 August 1988.

237 Hearings were formal but deliberately different from the style of a court. Everyone there, parent(s), child, reporter and social worker all sat around the same table; no police were present, and lawyers, rarely, as legal aid was not available.

238 Members of the group included Denise Platt, then President of the ADSS; John Harding, Chief Probation Officer for London; and Harry Fletcher of the National Association of Probation Officers.

239 Letter, LF to Don Brand, 13 November 1979. Patrick Jenkin was then Secretary of State at the DHSS.

240 Family Law, Comment, 18 February 1988, p. 41.

241 Nigel Parton, *Governing the Family*, (Basingstoke: Macmillan, 1991), Ch. 6.

242 *A Child in Trust: The Report of the Panel of Inquiry into the Circumstances Surrounding the Death of Jasmine Beckford,* London Borough of Brent. 1985 was a year of reports into other tragic child deaths, notably those of Tyra Henry in Lambeth, and Heidi Koseda. There followed, in 1987, the inquiry into the death of Kimberley Carlile in Greenwich.

243 The APPGC still exists, serviced by the National Children's Bureau, with the aim of raising awareness of children's issues both within and outside Parliament.

244 HL Deb. 20 December 1988 Vol. 502 c. 1333.

245 Over the course of a few months, two paediatricians diagnosed sexual abuse in 121 children from 57 families in the area. Most of the

children were removed from their homes under place of safety orders. This caused a national outcry. It came at a time when professionals were waking up to the existence of child sexual abuse. The enquiry into the scandal was chaired by Dame Elizabeth Butler-Sloss.

[246] HL Deb. 23 January 1989 Vol.503 c. 519.

[247] HL Deb. 7 February 1989 Vol. 503 c. 1448.

[248] On one occasion, puzzlingly, and to the anger of her many associates outside the House, Lucy voted against an amendment by Baroness David to give Local Authorities the duty to provide financial assistance, advice and support to care leavers 'in the manner of a good parent' [HL Deb. 17 January 1989 Vol. 503 c. 138]. The vote came after the Lord Chancellor had presented elaborate arguments about why the amendment was not necessary. Maybe Lucy wanted to toe the party line on this occasion. When she herself later introduced another similar amendment she said, "While supporting [Baroness David's] amendment in principle, I voted against it because I could not agree with the phrase 'in the manner of a good parent' because in our mixed ethnic society the concept of a good parent differs among the various groups" [HL Deb. 7 February 1989 Vol. 503 c. 1455]. I find this a particularly unconvincing excuse.

[249] HL Deb. 7 February 1989 Vol. 503 c. 1456.

[250] HL Deb. 7 February 1989 Vol. 503 c. 1460.

[251] HL Deb. 14 May 1990 Vol. 519 c. 134.

[252] The NCB had been established in 1963. It is associated in the public mind with the National Development Study, which followed 17,000 children born in one week in March 1956.

[253] Personal communication.

[254] Personal communication.

[255] John Rea Price, tape transcription of interview, 19 September 2005.

[256] 'Concern', Quarterly Magazine of the NCB. No. 68, Spring 1989.

[257] Barbara Wootton had been chair of London Juvenile courts for 16 years, and Professor of Social Studies at Bedford College, University of London. She was created one of the first life peers in 1958, and became deputy speaker of the House of Lords. Like Lucy, she was active into her eighties. She died in 1964.

[258] Personal communication

[259] She was particularly glad she did not accept, because Lucy died soon afterwards, the house was sold, and Daphne would have been homeless. Personal communication.

[260] Quoted by kind permission of Malcolm Gough.

[261] One of her (female) cousins, Gail Faithfull, was ordained in the American Episcopal Church. LF had mixed views about women priests.

[262] Letter, LF to Peter Smith, 25 July 1990. APPGC archive, National Children's Bureau.
[263] Letter, 26 February 1994. Inglewood Health Farm is at Kentbury, nr Hungerford, Berks
[264] Letter, Elizabeth Butler-Sloss to LF, 24 June 1992.

CHAPTER EIGHT

LADY FAITHLESS:
THE TROUBLESOME TORY

Juvenile justice

The Conservative Party has a long history of largely failed punitive policies designed to deal with young people who commit crimes, and Lucy had a personal history of opposing these policies of her own party. A typical Lucy contribution to debate came in November 1978:

> On the one hand, there are those who in panic reaction and revulsion cry for punishment, retribution and custodial care; on the other hand, there are those who view the young offender as one whose development has gone wrong and for whom an individual and imaginative remedy must be found. I believe that it is possible to give knowledgeable, compassionate and individual care to each delinquent child, establishing a relationship with them and at the same time providing discipline, structure and training.[265]

In 1980, Willie Whitelaw had won applause at the Tory party conference calling for a "short, sharp shock" for young offenders with "drill, parades and inspections". A White Paper of October that year, after the Tories had won the election, fulfilled the manifesto commitment to get tough, proposing the setting up of two pilot schemes at Send and New Hall with tougher regimes for children than at the existing detention centres. Lucy became quite the media star in the autumn of 1980. She was interviewed for the BBC TV programme *Newsweek* arguing that Detention Centres had been going for years and had not reduced juvenile crime, that support and help for young people and their families in the community was more effective, and that she regretted that the government was proposing to waste so much money on this scheme.[266] She also appeared with Lord Elwyn-Jones[267] in a Granada Television programme called *You, the Jury* on the subject of Detention Centres. She maintained that, by the end of the programme, 60% of those present had swung away from the idea of Detention Centres to supporting alternative care for juvenile offenders.

In June 1982, the Lords were debating one of many Criminal Justice Bills. Lucy summed up the situation within the government:

> Far be it from me to liken two great Government Departments, the Home Office and the Department of Health & Social Security, to Tweedledum and Tweedledee, but on juvenile delinquency they seem not to agree [...] On the one hand, there is the view of the DHSS, which lays emphasis on the principle of non-custodial care, supervision and care of the young delinquents in their own homes, in foster homes and in residential homes in the areas where they live [...] On the other hand, the Home Office lays emphasis on penal custodial care, the introduction of short detention centre orders, residential care orders and youth custody orders.

The Home Office punitive approach was indeed soon seen to be ineffective. That same year, Borstals were closed, and 'short sharp shock' regimes abolished by the same Tory government, who at that point called them "an expensive way of making bad people worse." Research showed that, between 1982 and 1992, offences by 10- to 16-year-olds fell by one third and that, between 1987 and 1992, young men under the age of 17 who were locked up re-offended significantly more than those who had received a community sentence. In 1992, under Kenneth Clarke's rule at the Home Office, Britain had a higher proportion of its population in prison than any other of the twelve EU states, with the exception of Portugal. Clarke repealed two sections of the 1991 Criminal Justice Act which was seen as too lenient.[268]

Then came the riot at Strangeways Prison, and the report by Lord Woolf calling for various liberal reform measures. The Tories were having none of this. In 1993, Michael Howard became Home Secretary. At the Conservative Party Conference in October that year, he put forward a twenty-one-point plan to "punish the wrong-doer and put the interests of the victim above those of the criminal". He was interviewed on the BBC TV *Newsnight* programme on 30th January 1994. This was the notorious occasion when he refused over and over to answer Jeremy Paxman's question "Do you think Lord Woolf was right or wrong?" It was around this time that Prime Minister John Major declared that it was "time to sweep away the fog of fashionable theories and get back to basics". Against all the evidence, Major staunchly maintained that "prison does work". Lucy herself was on TV, in a Channel 4 programme,[269] speaking on alternatives to custody for 12- to 14-year-olds. This prompted a deluge of correspondence from viewers and listeners.

Michael Howard's new Criminal Justice and Public Order Bill proposed the setting up of five "secure training centres", in effect mini-prisons, to be built across the country in the grounds of adult prisons, to lock up young children between the ages of twelve and fourteen. During the whole of 1994, Lucy was campaigning tirelessly against this Bill. She was, of course, vehemently opposed to any inhuman treatment of young people. The cost of these centres would be in the region of thirty million pounds a year for five years. This money could be better spent, she argued, on intervening with families at an earlier stage. Even worse, in Lucy's view, they were to be run by the private sector, which had no experience in the field. She found the idea of making money from locking up children abhorrent.

She knew that an effective system for the secure accommodation of young offenders was already in existence, run by Local Authorities, under the Department of Health, whereby children were accommodated geographically near to their families and so work could also be done with parents. She maintained that the proposed mini-prisons would be not only expensive but also wasteful. There was no need for another, parallel system for the incarceration of juveniles, which would, in any case, be ineffective and overly harsh because children would be placed miles away from their home networks.

She argued fiercely within her own party against Michael Howard's proposals. She thought he had miscalculated the number of young people needing secure accommodation. In January, she wrote a despairing letter to Frances Crook, of the Howard (no relation) League for Penal Reform, telling her that she had an appointment to take a deputation from New Approaches to Juvenile Crime to see the Home Secretary. Michael Howard was certainly not one of her favourite people, and she writes:

> I have little expectation that he will listen to me! One of our greatest problems is the fact that he states his scheme is supported by both the Magistrates Association and the Police. There is, I think, confusion. We all agree there must be adequate secure beds throughout the country. In my experience it is the need for secure beds which is causing the real problem at the moment in that the Local Authorities have not been able to set this up. I hope the Magistrates Association and Police can put this matter right with the Home Secretary.

We see her doing her homework, gathering her ammunition. In March, she writes to Chris Hanvey at The Thomas Coram Foundation mentioning that Gillian Wagner[270] had told her that the Coram Foundation had done research showing that 12- to 14-year-old children could be "dealt with in the community". She asks for details of this research, and adds, "I am being pressed by a tremendous number of Peers to know what this scheme is."[271] She asks the Dartington Social Research Unit for accurate figures of the number of crimes committed by the 12-14 age group; she writes to John Major at length setting out her reservations about Part 1 of the Bill, and explaining why, in its present form, she must oppose it. At an ADSS conference in Scotland she is seen ensconced in corners of the hotel with Scottish Directors gathering evidence of the superiority of the Scottish way of dealing with young offenders. This is typical of her way of operating – taking every opportunity of informing herself, gaining ammunition under the cover of a seemingly innocuous occasion. When the day of the appointment came her low expectations were fulfilled. I think it was on this occasion that she walked into Michael Howard's office. "I know why you've come", he is reported to have said, "and the answer's no."[272] In April 1994, she made a major speech in the Lords, referring to this meeting, and commenting, with a degree of sarcasm, that, "the Home Secretary is to be congratulated on achieving a grant of £30 million from the Treasury. Surely this sum, which is to be spent on [only] 100 children, should be used in ways that would go far to diminish juvenile crime?" She insisted, against House of Lords convention, on a Division on the amendment under discussion.[273]

She seems to have had a large part in the planning of a 1994 BBC *Panorama* programme[274] on the issue. She is seen sitting on a sofa interviewing the then Chief Probation Officer of London, John Harding, and, rather incongruously dressed in a large and stylish winter hat, touring a youth motor project in Walthamstow. She is then filmed standing on a prison balcony explaining to the viewer why locking up children is ineffective.

She told Daphne Statham about a time when, completely against parliamentary protocol, she stole into the Commons under cover of a division bell, and with people milling around, nobbled Tony

Blair on the mini-prison issue. She had heard that he was in favour of the secure units, and lurked in wait for him in his outer office, armed with all her evidence and statistics. She was in with him for some time, and when she came out she realised that it was not a safe time to return to the Lords, so she pretended to be a little old lady needing a cup of tea, which she was given while she waited for a more opportune moment to slip away. She wrote a letter to *The Times*, and even suggested to Simon Jenkins of *The Guardian* that he write a piece about the Bill.[275] A letter to her friend Lord Peyton of Yeovil, "My dear John", puts down in detail the actions she took behind the scenes to try to modify the Bill.

A crucial debate on Clause 1 of the Criminal Justice Bill was fixed in the House of Lords for Thursday, May 12th 1994. Lucy had marshalled all her forces, and the Bishops were to turn out in ranks of purple. On the Wednesday evening she took part in a television *Newsnight* panel discussion. Jeremy Paxton introduced her as the 'leader of the Lords revolt' against the government. She put her arguments against the mini-prisons articulately, but was smilingly embarrassed when Paxton challenged her, "Do you reckon you will defeat the government tomorrow?" "I hope I will, I'll see what happens", she answered.[276] But it was on that very Thursday that Labour Leader John Smith suddenly died. "We would have won the amendment", Lucy laments, but Parliament was prorogued, the debate was cancelled, and rescheduled. On the next appointed day, she writes, "twenty of the bishops who had been coming the previous Thursday could not manage the following Monday, and several other people had appointments in Strasbourg and Brussels".[277] She writes to Jenny Fells,

> We won the argument but lost the vote. [Firstly,] the
> Conservative Whip rang up every possible Peer [...] and
> many turned up that we rarely see. Secondly, it was felt to
> be a most unwise move for the House of Lords to cut out
> a whole Part of a Bill when the House of Commons had
> passed it [...] Several of the Peers came to me afterwards
> and said that this was the only reason why they voted

Lucy Faithfull: mother to hundreds

against the amendment, and that for the rest of the Bill they would support me.[278]

She had in fact been 'sent for' with a view to persuading her not to divide the House, but she had not given in. Amongst her papers I found a graceful letter she wrote to Lord Wakeham, then Leader of the House of Lords, apologising for being such a nuisance. She politely thanks him for his help:

> despite the fact that I must have caused you much concern and presented difficulties in my opposition to the Criminal Justice and Public Order Bill. I do understand that I did not make life easy for you, and for this I must apologise. I do, however, have to say that I still think that with regard to the children's prisons our Party's policy is misguided.[279]

In September she was still preoccupied with the issue. She wrote to Lord Robin Ferrers, (Minister of State at the Home Office), "I am so convinced that Part 1 of the Bill will in the end bring opprobrium on our Party that I felt I had to oppose the Home Secretary."[280] She was certainly not giving up her principles, her concern for her party's credibility, and, above all, her concern for children's welfare.

Lucy herself, as this affair of the Criminal Justice Bill (and her embarrassment on *Newsnight*) shows, had uncertainties and ambivalences about her stance in regard to her own party. She is reported as calling her position as one of being "loyally disloyal". Her document "Loyalty in the House of Lords" contains a revealing paragraph; in effect it is an apologia for her stance:

> *What is loyalty?* To vote for one's Party even if the policy is mis-guided and ill-advised does not seem to me to be loyal to the Party or [Country?]. In the House of Lords there are Peers who have qualified in one sphere or another, who have done a life-time's work and, therefore, judge policies on knowledge and experience. When, based on that knowledge and experience one challenges a

misguided policy this surely cannot be termed disloyalty. It is surely loyalty in the long run.

She goes on to discuss further examples where her conscience and experience has led her to oppose her own party.

Lucy's other major rebellions against her party were on a variety of issues.

The abolition of the Greater London Council.

From 1983, Margaret Thatcher's government made efforts to abolish the GLC and other Metropolitan authorities, in an effort to undermine the power of Labour in local government. Lucy was loyal to her ex-employer. In a debate Lucy mentions that she was once employed by the LCC. Her tentativeness in opposing her party on this issue is illustrated by a burst of self-deprecatory statements:

> I speak with enormous diffidence in that I feel like an inexperienced David taking on three Goliaths: the noble and Learned Lord, Lord Denning, my noble friend Lord Broxbourne, and my noble friend Lord Boyd-Carpenter. But I think there is an opposite view to be put.[281]

The Community Charge

In 1988, there was a major revolt in the House of Lords about the proposed Community Charge, or Poll Tax as it was commonly known. The Government hauled in all the 'backwoodsmen' who, in the normal run of things, rarely attended the House, resulting in the second largest attendance in the twentieth century. Lucy was among the seventeen Conservative peers opposing the Community Charge. A newspaper cutting from the time reports, "A group of senior Conservative peers are set to defy the government next week by tabling amendments to band the proposed poll tax to take account of people's ability to pay", thus easing the burden on the poor, which was Lucy's concern. It continues, "Mrs Thatcher is expected to hold her annual party for her peers on May 18, several months earlier than normal – to try to deter potential rebels". Despite this rebellion, she reported that Mrs Thatcher never once tried to bring her into line. "I went to see her several times and talked things over, but at no time did she tell me off for opposing the party".[282] Riots about the tax followed in March 1990, leading, some feel, to the downfall of Margaret Thatcher, and in April 1991 it was replaced by the Council Tax, under her successor, John Major.

The Child Support Act 1991

In an era of public spending cuts, this Act sought to reduce the ever increasing demands on the Income Support system by setting up the Child Support Agency, a deeply unpopular move. Lucy wrote to Michael Portillo, then Chief Secretary to the Treasury, telling him that in 1985 she had asked Mrs Thatcher to devote more resources into the over-pressed social security offices, whose staffing was inadequate in the face of increasing unemployment. She continued:

> I do have to say that the expense of administering the Child Support Act runs into millions of pounds [...]. Had the social security offices been helped in 1985 the expenditure on this Act would not have been necessary.[283]

Her diplomatically expressed view was, "as a Conservative I am strongly of the opinion that we must cut back our expenditure, but to make short-term cuts which in the end are going to be more costly, seems to me to an unwise method of dealing with the situation".[284]

Asked if it hadn't been difficult to fly in the face of her party so many times she answered, "Part of one's duty, I believe, as a responsible party member, is to use one's knowledge to save it from embarking on policies which are misguided or ill-advised".[285] It is significant that Lucy carefully preserved an article that appeared in

The Times newspaper for 13 June 1992 entitled, "Labour's working peers outstrip their Tory opponents." It gives the background to the concept of a working peer. Mrs Thatcher sometimes brought in talented outsiders, it notes, and sometimes her 'workers' in the upper house rebelled. It continues: "Baroness Faithfull is the most feared peer on the Tory side because, so the whip's lore goes, when she rebels, the government is likely to be defeated, such is her standing on social issues." She was regarded with some trepidation by the Whips who tended to ask her ruefully as she walked past, "Are we Lady Faithfull today, or Lady Faithless?"

Despite her reputation for not toeing the party line, Lucy remained in the circle of Margaret Thatcher. Her archive contains many letters from Mrs Thatcher on a range of issues. A typical one reads, "I know you have thought deeply about the reorganisation of local government and that you would not lightly have written to me about your reservations."[286] One evening at a party at 10 Downing Street, (perhaps the one designed to deter the Poll Tax rebels) a footman tapped Lucy on the shoulder and whispered that Princess Margaret, who was upstairs, would like to see her. Lucy climbed the stairs, knocked at the door, and, after several minutes with no response, went into the room, to find the Princess sitting with her feet up on the windowsill, smoking a cigarette. Lucy cleared her throat two or three times. There was still no response. "You wished to see me, Ma'am?" she queried. Whereupon Princess Margaret got up and left the room. Lucy had been in breach of protocol – you do not speak to a royal until you are spoken to.[287]

Family Law Bill – Mediation

In the autumn of 1995, the House of Lords was much preoccupied with the Family Law Bill, which controversially introduced the concept of "no-fault" divorce on the grounds of "irretrievable breakdown of marriage". Lucy was a strong supporter. She argued fiercely against Lord Simon of Glaisdale who thought that the Bill would make divorce too easy, and even against her friend and sponsor Dame Janet Young who is famous (or notorious according

Lucy Faithfull: mother to hundreds

to one's viewpoint) for her advocacy of the traditional family. In this, Lucy had the support of the Bishop of Oxford. "It is wise that the Bill drops the fault clause", Lucy said:

> Only in extreme cases can anyone outside the marriage judge where fault lies [...] and for the fault clause to be proved requires an adversarial system of wife versus husband or vice versa. Research by both Great Ormond Street Hospital and the Rowntree Trust shows that children's happiness, well-being and behaviour reflect the state of mind of the parents.

In acrimonious divorces, parents are 'overwrought', and this affects children "thereafter and long thereafter". The adversarial system mitigates against the "peaceful relationship necessary if children are to be in touch with both parents".[288]

In January 1996, she was still at it, talking from her own experience:

> The cruelty caused by adversarial divorce is appalling. A child came into my office one day with tears streaming down his face. I said 'Robert, what is the matter?' He said, 'They say my dad's a cad. I love my dad, and he is not a cad'. What had happened? The husband had left the wife, temporarily it turned out.[289]

She went on, uncharacteristically for her, to mention her faith. "I belong to the Church of England; there is such a thing as forgiveness."

She carefully explains the difference between reconciliation by marriage guidance when a marriage is in danger, and mediation after it has broken down. As Patron of the National Family Mediation Service she argues for funding for mediation (rather than adjudication) to help resolve issues such as 'access' after divorce. As she often did, she draws on her Social Work experience:

> I speak with very deep feeling because for two years I had to be in every Sunday evening when a father refused to

return his children to their mother after an access visit. I had to go and fetch the children, quite rightly, because it was the court's order that they should be brought back.[290]

In the face of Lord Mackay's reservations as to whether they should be funded by legal aid Lucy, unsuccessfully, emphasised the professionalism and training of the mediators.

Lucy absolutely loved being in the House of Lords 'club', and even in the face of political differences, most people there loved her back. She invited all her friends and contacts, at one time or another, for lunch or tea at the Palace of Westminster, some of them on a frequent basis. Dick Clough, General Secretary of the Social Care Association, was one of the people who had regular discussions with her. Simon Rodway reports that she was warm with everyone there regardless of rank. Waiting staff would do anything for her. They'd greet her, "Hello, my Lady, how are you today?" Dick Clough remembers that on one occasion she had left an alarm clock in her bag which went off in the middle of a debate. Anyone else would have been in deep trouble, but she was able to smile at the Sergeant at Arms, who remonstrated gently, "Oh, my Lady!" She could be a great gossip, although everyone agrees this was never malicious. I suspect she

Lucy Faithfull

could let her hair down with close friends such as Simon and Dick. Simon tells the tale of her pointing out Lord Archer across the tea room, "a dreadful man". Then Archer comes over to Lucy's table, "Oh, hello Jeffrey, how are you?" she says, all sweetness.

Her conference-going and other public events continued. 1995 was celebrated as the centenary of social work. Mary Stewart, the first hospital almoner, had begun work at the Royal Free Hospital on January 21st 1895. It was Lucy who unveiled a plaque at the hospital to mark the event and launch the celebration year. She was the main speaker, together with Ray Wyre of the Faithfull Foundation, at that year's British Association of Social Workers' Annual Study Course ('Conflict, Violence and Crisis: Social Work Solutions') at the Bedford Hotel, Brighton in early April. She was invited to preach the University Sermon for the 1994/5 academic year. She wrote to the Vice-Chancellor: "I am somewhat daunted at the thought of speaking to such a prestigious congregation, particularly as I do not regard myself as an academic".[291]

Northern Ireland

Over the years, Lucy maintained her links with Northern Ireland, crossing the Irish sea many times for conferences on various topics. In May 1992, she was asked over to speak as the Province was planning an Order based on the Children Act 1989. She writes:

> The Day Conference was held at Stranmills Teacher Training College, Belfast. It was well organised and had teachers, social workers, health visitors, psychologists, one psychiatrist and the Belfast BBC were there, also members of the civil service. It was clear that in the Province there are not the opportunities for those 'on the ground' to make known their views on legislation.[292]

She, and the All-Party Parliamentary Group for Children, campaigned against the introduction of Health and Social Services Trusts in Northern Ireland. In her capacity of chair of the All-Party Group she wrote to Lord Arran, Northern Ireland minister, setting out reservations.[293] She was particularly concerned that the acute health sector would dominate the budgets to the detriment of social services, and she questioned the idea that the hospital trust model was appropriate for community personal social services. A news item in the journal *Care Weekly* reported:

> Pressure from the APPGC has forced the Northern Ireland office to extend the consultation period on the establishment of health and social service trusts [...] after meeting a delegation led by the group's chairwoman, Baroness Faithfull.[294]

The Liberal Democrat peer, Baroness Seear later paid tribute, in the *Lords Diary*, to Lucy's commitment:

> Lady Faithfull, who never misses an opportunity to come to the rescue of children – surely 'mother to hundreds and nobody's wife' as the old song goes – asked me to meet representatives of voluntary organisations in Northern Ireland working for the well-being of children in the Province and especially families with children. Not surprisingly the children of Northern Ireland are more impoverished and more disabled than children anywhere else in the UK.[295]

Video evidence

In her last months in the House of Lords Lucy returned to the issues of children being able to give evidence in court proceedings by video. Back in the mid 1980s, Dr Ron Davie of the National Children's Bureau had chaired an international conference on children in the justice system, and been impressed by the contribution by a young Cambridge lawyer, John Spencer, who contended that the widespread belief that children's evidence was often unreliable, and that they were incapable of distinguishing between truth and falsehood, was unfounded and had no empirical evidence to support it. Spencer spoke at a meeting of the All-Party Parliamentary Group, and Lucy subsequently networked both in the House, and among social services contacts, and a number of high profile lawyers became convinced that children's evidence could in fact be relied upon. In 1990, a Home Office Advisory Group, the Pigot Committee, had advocated that a video recording be admissible as evidence in chief (with an informal pre-trial hearing for cross examination). The idea was to avoid altogether the appearance of child witnesses at the criminal trials of alleged perpetrators of sexual and physical abuse. Many eminent and Tory lawyers considered that this would interfere too much with the rights of the defendant. Lucy, of course, prioritised the interests of children. In another letter to Home Secretary Michael Howard, this time on behalf of APPGC, she had written politely:

> We were much concerned when in the Criminal Justice Bill 1991 the recommendations of the [Pigot] Report were not fully implemented. We would wish to seek your advice as to the action we should take with your approval to implement the Pigot Report recommendations in full.

No doubt steeling herself, she had asked for another meeting with Howard.[296] She also lobbied hard on this issue in her role as Chairman of the Family Courts Campaign. In this, she was supported by her friend, the Labour Peeress Baroness Nora David, who had been an ally during the 1988 Children Bill debates. In the face of doubts expressed by Baroness Blatch, the Minister of State at the Home office, she suggested an inter-disciplinary meeting, "between now and the third reading" because "it seems to me that we are not listening to the people who are doing the work, namely the social services workers, voluntary organisations, and many judges and QCs."[297]

Death and afterlife

On 12 March 1996, just after chairing a meeting of social work colleagues to consider how to celebrate the upcoming fiftieth anniversary of the 1948 Children's Act, Lucy suddenly collapsed in a corridor of the House of Lords. Simon Rodway of Caldecott was holding her arm when she said, "There's something funny happening to me", and slid down onto the floor. She was only unconscious for a short time. First aid help was summoned, but took ages coming, and, meanwhile, various peers came past along the corridor. Janet Young's not very sensitive comment was, "You can't die Lucy; I appointed you." More sympathetic was Lord Longford, who asked Simon, "Do you think I could give her a kiss?" A sweet thought. Simon Rodway and Jane Tunstill from Royal Holloway stayed with her as she was taken by ambulance across the Thames to St Thomas' Hospital. A young doctor bounced up, inappropriately calling her "Lucy", and started to undress her in front of Simon and Jane. They hastily withdrew, and then waited five or six hours for her. The doctors could find nothing wrong. She seemed to recover, Simon called a taxi and they were escorting her out of the hospital when she collapsed again. She was admitted overnight for 'observation', and given a bed by a window overlooking the Thames and the Houses of Parliament.

Her Wimbledon hosts, the Holdens, rushed to see her early the next day, but were not allowed into her room. Her end came quickly. She died that morning of an undiagnosed thrombosis. On admission she had designated her distant cousin, Hugh Faithfull, who is also a social worker, as her next of kin, and it was he who received the phone call informing him of her death.

Simon feels that, towards the end, Lucy was beginning to lose her touch: she was forgetting names, getting things wrong, and had perhaps hung on too long. Her friend and surgeon, Malcolm Gough agrees. She had had a fall in 1992 (in the bath at some conference hotel), and he had also noticed that her ankles were swelling. He had sent her a present of money for a car phone. "You really should have one, as you insist on doing these long drives to and from London," he told her.[298] He felt she was not taking good care of herself, perhaps realising that her time was near. On the day of her death, Simon phoned around the other Caldecott trustees to tell them the news. The wife of one member, before he could get to the point, blurted out, "Simon, you must do something about

Lucy Faithfull: mother to hundreds

Lucy, it's dreadful, you must stop her being a trustee". "Well, that is what I want to speak to x about", Simon replied. "Nature has intervened".

Perhaps Lucy died at the right time.

Later that same morning, 13 March 1996, up in the small Scottish town of Dunblane, a paedophile gunman walked into a primary school and shot dead several young children. Many people, knowing how agonised she would be, felt relief that Lucy never had to know about this terrible event. Others, knowing of her quiet faith, felt that she had been called to take care of the many small children who died that day.

In the House of Lords there was shock at both events. Lord Richard spoke for many when he said:

> My Lords, it is not usual in this House for there to be tributes to Members who are Back-Benchers. I am told that tributes are reserved for nominally more exalted beings. However for every rule there is an exception. Therefore I hope that the House will allow me to say one or two words upon the death of Lady Faithfull.

> We were deeply saddened at the news of her sudden death. She was a colleague and, across the party divide, a friend. As I sat on this bench this morning my noble friend Lady Hollis said how strange it was to look across the Chamber and to see the noble Lord, Lord Peyton, but not see Lady Faithfull sitting next to him in the green suit she so often wore. It is particularly sad because yesterday she was actively playing her part in the House.

> In many ways Lady Faithfull was a Back-Bencher par excellence of this House. She pursued her causes with vigour, determination and a very considerable degree of single-minded independence. Her background in social work made her particularly effective in those areas of Parliament's work. She carved for herself a very special

and unique role [...] We shall all remember her for her independence, persistence, sense of humour, compassion, and most of all, her kindness.[299]

Some time earlier, at her flat in Woodstock Road, Lucy had planned her own funeral, with Canon Brian Mountford from the University Church of St Mary the Virgin, and the person she wanted to be her executor, her friend Malcolm Gough. The small, private, and very moving funeral took place at St. Mary's where she had been a regular attender for so many years. Malcolm Gough has some sympathy for Brian Mountford, who has to deal with the highly intellectual academic theologians who abound in Oxford. Gough finds Mountford open and kind, with a liberality of mind to match Lucy's. Although Lucy's funeral took place during the season of Lent, when traditionally churches are sombre and shrouded, Sheila Gough wanted to fill the place with daffodils from her garden, and Mountford kindly allowed this. Baroness Daphne Park gave a moving address, quoting Lucy's favourite quotation from *Hamlet*, Polonius saying:

> To thine own self be true, and it must follow, as the night the day,
> Thou canst not then be false to any man.

She went on:

> This small, courageous woman, proud to be a grandchild of missionaries, a doughty defender of the weak and crusader for what she believed, often an opponent but never an enemy, lived according to that precept.

Malcolm Gough approached Mountford with the hope that a plaque could be erected at St Mary's in memory of Lucy, but the vicar replied that she used to sit in the chancel where there was very ancient wood paneling that could not be damaged. Also that there were other claims on behalf of a recently deceased churchwarden, and, in any case, the whole matter was "governed by very strict Faculty legislation",[300] so that idea came to nothing.

A few weeks later, Hugh Faithfull, conscious of his role as 'next of kin', visited Oxford, had tea with Malcolm and Sheila Gough, and went to collect Lucy's ashes from the undertaker. He and his wife Jenny scattered them on the banks of the canal behind her house in Woodstock Road. This is the area where she had scattered her brother's ashes years before, so Hugh thinks she had left specific instructions that this is where she wanted to be.

Soon after the Oxford funeral there was a huge and impressive Memorial Service at St Margaret's, Westminster. Lucy's friends Lord John Peyton and Daphne Park were involved in the arrangements. Daphne was very keen to have Parry's *Jerusalem* played. She felt that the contrasts between the "dark satanic mills" and the "bow of burning gold" were so appropriate to the contrasts in Lucy's life, but the Chaplain to the Speaker ("a horrid man") would not allow it. There were huge numbers of Lords, and representatives of the many organisations and charities with which she was connected, all listed in detail in *The Times* of 7 June. Hugh Faithfull had a moment of glory as chief mourner, but Lucy's American cousins, Lucia and the Reverend Gail, with whom she had spent so many happy summer holidays, were not there. Malcolm Gough read from a poem he had found on a much thumbed piece of paper folded up in the prayer book beside Lucy's bed, "Pray When the Morn is Breaking [...]" He did not know who had written this, or where it came from, but later learned the words were from a hymn. Lucy's friend Lord John Peyton gave an address, and "his words are eloquent testimony to the effect Lucy produced on people who had had little previous understanding of the causes she championed".[301] Lord Peyton said she had told him that, in order to achieve 'a relationship of lasting value, a social worker must surely have touched the garment of God', something which he thought she surely achieved. He goes on:

> Lucy was first and last a social worker, a role which she
> so lit up as to make it at least the equal of any other. Her
> concern for the vulnerable, the lonely and the dying was
> an imperative and a source of almost unceasing energy;

children unloved, neglected, abused and damaged were her especial care. She enjoyed the House of Lords, which did not, in her view, stand in quite such urgent need of reform as some now suggest. She respected it, and she was angry when a rather tiresome person with one of those in-built sneers which are the fashion of our time set out to trivialise it in a film made for television. She welcomed and used to the full the opportunities which the House of Lords gave her to speak for those whose voices are barely audible above the din of modern times.

It was characteristic of her to want to share such an institution with people, particularly the young, who might not otherwise see it. On one occasion, a number of those whom she had come to know through their problems – she called them 'my children' – arrived on a visit. A watchful attendant pointed out to her that they were all chewing gum, a habit not generally indulged in within those precincts. She issued instructions that the chewing should cease and was at once obeyed. Reflecting upon this later, and wondering what had happened to the gum, she went back along the route which the group had taken and retrieved a quantity of it from various places in which it had been hurriedly stowed away.[302]

Although Lucy had wanted to appoint Malcolm Gough as her executor, she never in fact altered her will to bring this about. The formality of administering the will[303] was left to the impersonal attentions of the National Westminster Bank. She left money to the many charities she was involved with. Among more personal things, she had specified that her family silver should go to Malcolm and Sheila Gough, but it had been taken from her flat in an upsetting burglary in the late eighties. There was one silver tray which she left to her Godson Adam White, (perhaps one of 'her' children in Care?). She left her jewellery to another friend, Mary Whitton Davies. Lucy had taken Mary on some of her cruise holidays, aware that Mary was under pressure because her husband, the Dean of Christchurch, suffered from Alzheimer's Disease. Lucy had loved amber, and for her 85th birthday, Sheila Gough had given her a ring she'd had made up with an amber inset, which Lucy had left to Daphne Park in her will. Daphne kindly gave it back to Sheila at her request.

After Lucy's death, Malcolm Gough approached many of the eminent people on the attendance list at the Memorial Service to raise money for The Lucy Faithfull Travel Scholarship Trust. He raised £52,000. Other trustees were Baroness Daphne Park, Professor Olive Stevenson and Judge Quentin Campbell, a judge in the family courts. The Trust was to fund two social workers (or children's doctors) a year to spend three months gaining practical experience or training abroad, and reporting back so others could benefit from their experiences. Two social workers were sponsored to go to the States, one went to Germany, and the Scholarship lasted for five years. Malcolm Gough found it time-consuming, organising the advertising and interviewing applicants. The fund was eventually wound up because of difficulties attracting applicants of the right calibre, and problems social workers had in getting leave of absence from their employers. Gough offered the remaining funds to Bessels Leigh School which, although grateful, never took up the offer. (Barbara Kahan was by now Chair of the Governors, which might explain the lack of response.) So the funds were donated to Helen House, a children's hospice in Oxford run by charismatic Sister Frances Dominica, with the request that it be used for postgraduate courses for carers.

Lucy had a very feminine way of making friends and influencing people. She took a stance of humbling herself, being a seeker of information from other people, showing genuine interest in people's views, seeking their help. She then stored up what she learned and used it to great effect when the moment arose. She would bring people together. She was always inviting people to lunch or tea at the Lords to meet each other. She used her extensive contacts either to influence people directly or to influence those she thought could influence. She disproved those male Directors of Social Services who, in 1974, wanted an intellectual heavyweight to represent them in the Lords, and doubted whether Lucy was the right person to be championing social work. She, as the woman she was, was "a damn sight more effective than any of those would have been", says Tom White.[304]

Among the tributes to Lucy after her death was one from Bob Holman. He picks on a small episode in her life, but one that illustrates so well the quality of her engagement with children and those involved with them. He writes that she:

> was one of the few great child care figures of [the 20th century]. She had the great gift of being adept at policy making, public speaking and personal communication. A few years ago she asked to visit Easterhouse[305] where I work. She went into the local primary school where she was immediately at home with the children, and left the teachers glowing with her interest and enthusiasm. Soon afterwards she sent a hand-written letter to the school saying how impressed she was with it. It went straight onto the notice board, for her comments were a tremendous boost to staff who served in a very deprived area with little recognition. Thank you, Lucy.[306]

Sir William Utting, who knew Lucy from his days as Chief Social Work Officer at the DHSS, sums up the essence of her being, "The whole of suffering humanity awakened her concern. I […] sensed that the inspiration for the love she shed about her lay in a profound Christian faith." He continues:

> Lucy set out to do good, and to that end deployed formidable qualities of persistence (I learned early on that it saved a great deal of time and trouble if one did something for Lucy the *first* time she requested it), backed by an inexhaustible supply of charm, and exercised fearlessly across an extraordinary network. The House of Lords provided the perfect stage for her activities, and

Lucy Faithfull: mother to hundreds

she exploited to the full the *entrée* her title afforded to every sector of potential influence. [...] Much of Lucy's influence was exercised through personal exchanges that were unrecorded except in the memories of those who shared them. In the end, it was who she was that mattered. Lucy was not perfect, but she possessed a fundamental goodness, and a dedication to doing good, that nearly all who met her recognised and responded to.[307]

This was Lucy Faithfull.

Notes:

[265] HL Deb. (Series 5) 7 November 1978 Vol. 396 c. 230.

[266] *Newsweek*: 'Young Offenders', 24 October 1980, British Film Institute archive.

[267] Frederick Elwyn Jones had been Lord Chancellor under the Labour government between 1974 and 1979. He was Lord of Appeal in 1980.

[268] In January 2008, after Lucy's death, in the context of yet another Criminal Justice Bill, Baroness Stern paid tribute to Lucy's past contributions. She was, she said, a Conservative peer of "immense achievements", and had been instrumental in limiting the circumstances in which a court could pass a custodial sentence on a young person under 21, resulting in a 54% reduction in the use of custody for young people.

[269] On 2 April 1994 at 8.30 p.m. She was also interviewed on BBC Radio 4's *Today* programme on 12 May.

[270] Gillian Wagner was, at the time, the Chair of the Coram Foundation, (now Coram Family), and is the biographer of its founder, Thomas Coram. She was made a Dame in 1994.

[271] Letter, LF to Gillian Wagner, 31 March 1994

[272] She told this story to her young cousin, Hugh Faithfull, who is also a social worker.

[273] HL Deb. (Series 5) 16 May 1994 Vol. 555 c. 56.

[274] Video taped by Prof. June Thoburn of the University of East Anglia.

[275] An anonymous Leader did appear, "Curbing Crime the Faithfull Way", *The Guardian*, 16 May 1994.

[276] *Newsnight*, 11 May 1994. British Film Institute archive.

[277] Letter, LF to Dr. Duncan Dolton 10 June 1994.

[278] Letter, LF to Jenny Fells, 26 May 1994.

[279] Letter, LF to Lord Wakeham, 30 July 1994.

[280] Letter, LF to Earl Ferrers.
[281] HL Deb. (Series 5) 18 February 1986 Vol. 471 c. 521.
[282] Simon Crompton, "Lucy Faithfull: The Reluctant Rebel", in *Professional Social Work*, (BASW: February 1995).
[283] Letter, LF to Michael Portillo, 1 October 1993.
[284] Ibid.
[285] Crompton, 1995.
[286] Letter, Margaret Thatcher to LF, 9 July 1984.
[287] This is another story that Lucy laughingly related to her cousin Hugh Faithfull.
[288] HL Deb. (Series 5) 30 November 1995 Vol. c.717.
[289] HL Deb. (Series 5) 11 January 1996 Vol. 568 c. 337.
[290] HL Deb. (Series 5) 23 January 1996 Vol. 568 c. 919.
[291] Letter, LF to Dr Peter North, 13 December 1994.
[292] Letter, LF to 'John', 28 May 1992. APPGC archive, National Children's Bureau.
[293] Letter, LF to The Earl of Arran, (undated). APPGC archive.
[294] *Care Weekly*, 29 July 1993.
[295] *The House Magazine*, Vol. 20, No. 667, 6 March 1995.
[296] Letter, LF to Michael Howard, 20 October 1993. APPGC archive, National Children's Bureau.
[297] HL Deb. (Series 5) 5 February 1996 Vol. 569 c. 99
[298] Letter, Malcolm Gough to LF, 5.January 1995.
[299] HL Deb. (Series 5) 13 March 1996 Vol. 570 cc. 848-91.
[300] Letter, Rev. Mountford to Malcolm Gough, 25 March 1996.
[301] Sir William Utting, personal communication. Bill Utting's main publication is "People Like Us", 1997, a review for the Government of the safeguards for children living away from home, a cause after Lucy's heart.
[302] John Peyton, *Without Benefit of Laundry: the autobiography of John Peyton*, (London: Bloomsbury, 1997). p. 206.
[303] She left £535,000, the greater part of which, according to Malcolm Gough, she had inherited from her brother.
[304] Tom White, tape transcription, interview 13 December 2006.
[305] Easterhouse is a housing estate in Glasgow.
[306] Tribute to LF in the *Family Support Network (UEA and Keele Universities) Newsletter* No. 5, Spring 1996.
[307] Sir William Utting, personal communication.

BIBLIOGRAPHY

Books

Abrams, Rebecca, *Woman in a Man's World: Pioneering career women of the twentieth century*, (London: Methuen, 1993).

Burn, Michael, *Mr Lyward's Answer*, (London: Hamish Hamilton, 1956).

Bowlby, John, *Child Care and the Growth of Love*, (Harmondsworth: Pelican, 1953).

Clarke, John, (ed.), *A Crisis in Care? Challenges to Social Work.* (London: Sage, 1993).

Evans, Ruth, *Happy Families: Recollections of a Career in Social Work.* (London: Peter Owen, 1977).

Glasby, Jon, *Poverty and Opportunity: 100 Years of the Birmingham Settlement*, (Studley: Brewin Books, 1999).

Hart, Matthew, *The Irish Game: A True Story of Crime and Art,* (New York: Walkerbooks, 2002).

Heywood, Jean S., *Children in Care*, (London: Routledge and Kegan Paul, 1959).

Herbert, A.P., *A Book of Ballads*, (London, Ernest Benn Ltd).

Holman, Bob, *The Evacuation: A Very British Revolution,* (Oxford: Lion Publishing, 1995).

--------------, *Champions for Children*, (Bristol: The Policy Press, 2001).

--------------, *Child Care Revisited: The Children's Departments 1948-1971*, (London: Institute of Child Care & Social Education UK, 1998).

Joel Kanter (ed.) *Face to Face with Children – The Life and Work of Clare Winnicott.* (London: Karnac, 2004).

Lawton, D. and P. Gordon, *HMI*, (London: Routledge & Kegan Paul, 1987).

Little, Michael (with Siobhan Kelly), A *Life Without Problems? The achievements of a therapeutic community*, (Aldershot: Arena, 1995).

Packman, Jean, *The Child's Generation*. 2ⁿᵈ Edition. (Oxford: Blackwell & Robertson, 1981).

Peyton, John, *Without Benefit of Laundry: the autobiography of John Peyton*, (London: Bloomsbury, 1997).

Ratcliffe, Eric, *The Caxton of her Age. The Career and Family Background of Emily Faithfull (1835-95)*, (Upton-upon-Severn: Images, 1994).

Rimmer, Joyce, *Troubles Shared: The Story of a Settlement 1899-1979* (Birmingham: Phlogiston Publishing, 1980).

Stroud, John, *The Shorn Lamb*, (Longmans, 1960).

Sym, Col. John (ed.), *Seaforth Highlanders*, (Aldershot: Gale & Polden Ltd, 1962).

Younghusband, Eileen, *Social Work in Britain 1950-1975*, (London: George Allen & Unwin, 1978).

Wyre, Ray, and Tim Tate, *The Murder of Childhood. Inside the mind of one of Britain's most notorious child murderers*, (London: Penguin, 1995).

Articles

Anon., "Curbing Crime the Faithfull Way", *The Guardian*, (16 May 1994.).

Crompton, Simon, "Lucy Faithfull: The Reluctant Rebel", in *Professional Social Work*, (British Association of Social Workers, February 1995)

Eldridge, H.J., and R. Wyre., "The Lucy Faithfull Foundation Residential Program for Sexual Offenders", in Marshall, W.L. et al. *Sourcebook of Treatment Programs for Sexual Offenders*. (New York: Plenum, 1998).

Faithfull, Lucy (subsequently revised.), "Younghusband, Dame Eileen Louise (1902-1981)", *Oxford Dictionary of National Biography,* (Oxford: OUP, 2004).

Holman, Bob, "The Evacuation: Children of the revolution fifty years ago next month". *The Guardian*, (12 April 1995).

---------------, "Warfare to Welfare" *Community Care* (5 May 2005).

Hughes, Rupert, "The Children Act 1948 and 1989: Similarities, differences, continuities" in *Child & Family Social Work*. **3** (1993), 149-153.

----------------, "Policy Networks in England and France: the case of child care policy 1980-1989" in *Journal of European Public Policy*. **7**, 2 (2000), 244-260.

Kay, Ernest (ed.), "Faithfull, Lucy", *World Who's Who of Women*, 11th ed., (Cambridge: International Biographical Centre, 1992).

Philpot, Terry, "Profile: Faithfull in her Fashion", *Community Care*, (20-27 December 1990), 16.

Rea Price, John, "Faithfull, Lucy, Baroness Faithfull (1910-1996)", *Oxford Dictionary of National Biography*, (Oxford: OUP, 2004).

Stevenson, Olive, "50 Years of services to children in need of care: What have we learnt for tomorrow?" Lucy Faithfull Memorial Lecture. St Anne's College, Oxford. (Barkingside: Barnardo's, 1997).

Thoburn, June, "Trends in Foster Care and Adoption", in Stevenson, Olive (ed.) *Child Welfare in the UK*, (Blackwell Science, 1998), 121.

Utting, Sir William, "A View from Central Government" in Davis, Martin (ed.), *The Blackwell Companion to Social Work*, (Oxford: Blackwell, 1997).

Winnicott, Donald, "The Nature of the Child's Tie to His Mother", *International Journal of Psycho-Analysis,* (1958).

Interviews

Olive Stevenson. Interviewed by Niamh Dillon, 2004-5. National Sound Archive, British Library.

Obituaries

(Anon.), "Baroness Faithfull", *The Times*, (14 March 1996).

(Anon.), "Baroness Faithfull", *The Daily Telegraph*, (14 March 1996).

Jackson, Sonia, "Baroness Faithfull 1910-1996", *British Journal of Social Work*. **26**, (1996) 447-450.

Philpot, Terry, "Baroness Faithfull", *The Independent*, (15 March 1996).

Rodway, Simon, "Tireless campaigner for children's needs: Baroness Faithfull", *The Guardian*, (14 March 1996).

INDEX